ESSENTIAL ELEMENTS
FOR BAND

W9-AYA-440

COMPREHENSIVE BAND METHOD

TIM LAUTZENHEISER   **JOHN HIGGINS**   **CHARLES MENGHINI**
PAUL LAVENDER   **TOM C. RHODES**   **DON BIERSCHENK**

Percussion consultant and editor
WILL RAPP

Band is… **M**aking music with a family of lifelong friends.
Understanding how commitment and dedication lead to success.
Sharing the joy and rewards of working together.
Individuals who develop self-confidence.
Creativity—expressing yourself in a universal language.
Band is…**MUSIC!**

Strike up the band,
Tim Lautzenheiser

HISTORY OF PERCUSSION

Percussion instruments were invented by prehistoric cultures. However, most percussion history is connected with military groups. Drums were used in the 700 A.D. Moorish invasion of Africa. These instruments were ancestors of the snare drum and timpani. Both the Scots and Swiss developed the snare drum around 1300.

Around 1450, Turkish military bands featured triangles, cymbals and several sizes of drums. The instruments used in these "Janizary Bands" communicated signals to large numbers of fighting troops.

J. S. Bach, Mozart, Beethoven, Berlioz, Debussy, Sousa and Stravinsky are all important composers who have included percussion in their writing.

Common percussion instruments are the snare drum, bass drum, crash cymbals, triangle and timpani. Famous percussionists include Vic Firth, Peter Erskine, Buddy Rich and Al Payson.

Student Activation Code
E1PC-5662-9590-8667

ISBN 978-0-634-00327-1

HAL•LEONARD®
CORPORATION
7777 W. BLUEMOUND RD. P.O. BOX 13819 MILWAUKEE, WI 53213

THE BASICS

Posture

Stand near your instrument, and always keep your:

- Spine straight and tall
- Shoulders back and relaxed
- Feet flat on the floor

Matched Grip (A Natural Stick Position)

Every percussion instrument requiring sticks or mallets can be played with this basic grip. Both sticks or mallets are held exactly the same "matched" way.

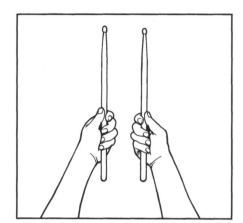

- Place the sticks in front of you with the tip of the sticks pointing forward.
- Extend your right hand as if shaking hands with someone.
- Pick up the right stick with your thumb and index finger about 1/3 from the end of the stick.
- The curve of your index finger's top knuckle and the thumb hold the stick in place, creating a pivot point.
- Gently curve your other fingers around the stick.
- Check to be sure the stick is cradled in the palm of your hand.
- Turn your hand palm-down to a comfortable resting position.
- Follow the same procedure for your left hand.

Practice & Performance Position

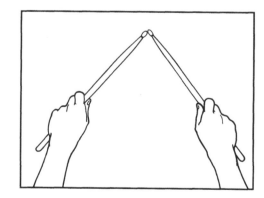

- Put the practice pad on a flat surface slightly below your waist.
- Stand up straight with your arms relaxed at your side. Raise your forearms by bending your elbows.
- Form the outline of a slice of pie with the sticks about 2 inches above the practice pad.
- Move your wrists to raise the sticks 6–8 inches from the practice pad. This is the "up" position.
- Begin with your right hand. Strike near the center using a quick, reflex-like wrist action. Let the stick return to the "up" position to prepare for the next strike.
- Follow with your left hand, and strike about 1 inch away from your first right hand strike. Return to the "up" position.
- When resting, keep the sticks about 2 inches above the practice pad in the outline of a slice of pie.

Sticking Work-Outs

R = Right hand stick
L = Left hand stick

Play the following sticking work-out on your practice pad, keeping an even pulse when playing and resting:

● = Strike near the center of the practice pad.

R	L	R	L		REST		R	L	R	L		REST
●	●	●	●				●	●	●	●		

You will learn several "sticking" methods in this book.
The method above is called **Right Hand Lead** (RLRL…RLRL, etc.).

Getting It Together

The two ways to set up the snare drum depend on which grip you are using. Matched Grip = level drum set-up.
Traditional Grip = angled drum set-up.

Step 1 Open the bottom legs of the snare drum stand. Lock them into place by tightening the tripod base screw. Grasp the bar and raise stand below your waist. Tighten the height adjustment screw and lock into place.

Step 2 Put the two support bars closest together in front of you. Be certain they are even. If your stand has an adjustable arm, it should point away from you and be extended. The bars should be parallel to the ground. Tighten the angle adjustment screw.

Step 3 Carefully place the snare drum in the stand so the snare strainer lever faces you.

Step 4 Slide the adjustable arm until it fits snugly against the shell of the drum. The top batter head should be slightly below your waist. Lock your drum stand into position. Tighten all screws each time you play.

Step 5 Tighten the snare strainer. Tap the head of the snare drum. If the sound is not crisp, tighten or loosen the tension control screw. The snares should rest lightly against the bottom head. Stand by the drum as shown:

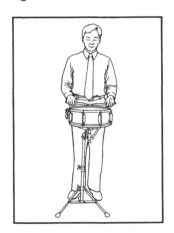

MATCHED GRIP SNARE DRUM SET-UP

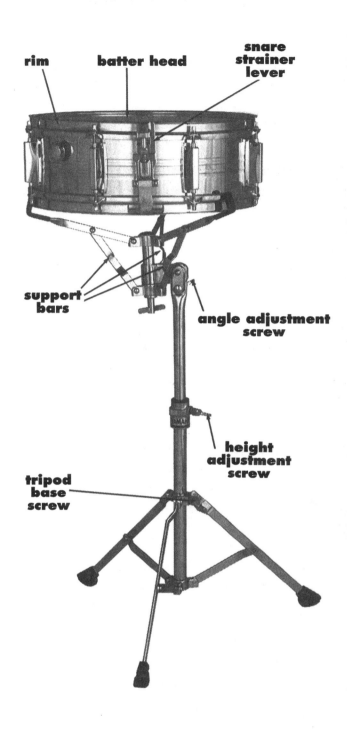

rim   batter head   snare strainer lever

support bars

angle adjustment screw

height adjustment screw

tripod base screw

READING MUSIC   Identify and draw each of these symbols:

Music Staff

The **music staff** has 5 lines and 4 spaces where notes and rests are written.

Ledger Lines

Ledger lines extend the music staff. Notes on ledger lines can be above or below the staff.

Measures & Bar Lines

Measure   *Measure*

Bar Line   *Bar Line*   *Bar Line*

Bar lines divide the music staff into **measures**.

THE BASICS

Posture

Stand near your instrument, and always keep your:

- Spine straight and tall
- Shoulders back and relaxed
- Feet flat on the floor

Traditional Grip

The traditional grip is another way to hold your snare drum sticks. Your teacher will tell you which grip you should use.

LEFT HAND

- Turn your left hand palm-down and open your fingers.
- With the tip pointing down, place the stick in the webbing of your thumb. About 1/3 – 1/4 of the stick should extend above the thumb.
- Turn your hand palm-up, and let the stick rest gently between your middle and ring fingers. The webbing of your thumb **holds** the stick in place. Your fingers simply **balance** it.
- The left forearm and wrist control the stick motion.

RIGHT HAND

- Follow the Matched Grip instructions on page 2 – Matched Grip.
- Check to be sure the sticks are cradled in the palm of your hand as shown:

Practice & Performance Position

- Put the practice pad on a flat surface slightly below your waist.
- Stand up straight with your arms relaxed at your side. Raise your forearms by bending your elbows.
- Form the outline of a large slice of pie with the sticks about 2 inches above the practice pad. Your left stick will be further away from your body than the right.
- Move your wrists to raise the sticks 6–8 inches from the practice pad. This is the "up" position.
- Beging with your right hand. Strike near the center using a quick, reflex-like wrist action. Let the stick return to the "up" position to prepare for the next strike.
- Follow with your left hand, and strike about 1 inch away from your first right hand strike. Return to the "up" position.
- When resting, keep the sticks about 2 inches above the practice pad or drum head in the outline of a large slice of pie.

Sticking Work-Outs

R = Right hand stick
L = Left hand stick
Play the following sticking work-out on your practice pad, keeping an even pulse when playing and resting:

● = Strike near the center of the practice pad.

R		L	R	L		REST		R		L	R	L		REST
●		●	●	●				●		●	●	●		

You will learn several "sticking" methods in this book.
The method above is called **Right Hand Lead** (RLRL…RLRL, etc.).

Getting It Together

The two ways to set up the snare drum depend on which grip you are using. Matched Grip = level drum set-up.
Traditional Grip = angled drum set-up.

Step 1 Open the bottom legs of the snare drum stand. Lock them into place by tightening the tripod base screw. Grasp the bar and raise stand below your waist. Tighten the height adjustment screw and lock into place.

Step 2 Put the two support bars closest together in front of you. Be certain they are even. Put the remaining support bar on your left and raise it about 2 inches. Tighten the angle adjustment screw.

Step 3 Carefully place the snare drum in the stand so the snare strainer lever faces you. The left side should be angled higher.

Step 4 Slide the adjustable arm until it fits snugly against the shell of the drum. The top batter head should be slightly below your waist. Lock your drum stand into position. Tighten all screws each time you play.

Step 5 Tighten the snare strainer. Tap the head of the snare drum. If the sound is not crisp, tighten or loosen the tension control screw. The snares should rest lightly against the bottom head. Stand by the drum as shown:

READING MUSIC

Identify and draw each of these symbols:

Music Staff

The **music staff** has 5 lines and 4 spaces where notes and rests are written.

Ledger Lines

Ledger lines extend the music staff. Notes on ledger lines can be above or below the staff.

Measures & Bar Lines

Measure　　　*Measure*

Bar Line　　*Bar Line*　　*Bar Line*

Bar lines divide the music staff into **measures**.

BASIC PERCUSSION INSTRUMENTS

Percussionists play several instruments. Snare drum and keyboard percussion instruments provide the basic techniques to play all other instruments in the percussion section. Ask your director to help you identify each of these basic percussion instruments and mallets you may have in your school's band room.

INSTRUMENT	MALLET/STICK
Concert Snare Drum with stand	5B or 2B sticks
Concert Bass Drum with stand	1 pair medium bass drum mallets
Crash Cymbals (16" to 18")	Played in pairs
Suspended Cymbal and stand (16" to 18")	1 pair medium yarn mallets
Triangle with clip	1 pair metal beaters
Wood Block	1 pair medium rubber mallets 1 pair hard rubber mallets
Timpani (23", 26", 29", 32")	1 pair general timpani mallets 1 pair hard timpani mallets
Bells	1 pair very hard lexan mallets 1 pair hard rubber mallets
Xylophone	1 pair hard rubber mallets 1 pair medium rubber mallets
Chimes	2 plastic or 2 rawhide mallets
Marimba	Various yarn and rubber mallets
Vibraphone	Various yarn and rubber mallets

General Accessories:
Tambourines (with and without head),
Cowbell, Bongos, Congas, Timbales,
Maracas, Guiro, Claves, Castanets,
Slapstick, Sleigh Bells, Slide Whistle.

The Beat

The **beat** is the pulse of music, and like your heartbeat it should remain very steady. Counting aloud and foot-tapping help us maintain a steady beat. Tap your foot **down** on each number and **up** on each "&."

One beat = 1 &
↓ ↑

Notes And Rests

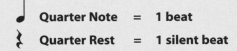

Notes tell us how high or low to play by their placement on a line or space of the music staff, and how long to play by their shape. **Rests** tell us to count silent beats.

♩ **Quarter Note** = 1 beat
𝄽 **Quarter Rest** = 1 silent beat

1. THE FIRST NOTE *Play your quarter note as the band plays their long tone.*

△ *Start with right-hand stick*

2. COUNT AND PLAY

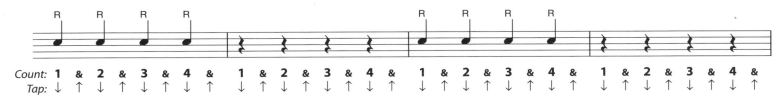

3. A NEW NOTE

△ *Play sticking as marked.*

4. TWO'S A TEAM

5. HEADING DOWN *Always stand straight and tall with your shoulders relaxed.*

6. MOVING ON UP

Clefs indicate a new line of music and a set of note names. Percussion instruments use three common clefs:

Percussion Clef

Snare Drum
Bass Drum
Cymbals
Drum Set
Accessory Instruments

Treble Clef

Bells
Xylophone
Marimba
Vibraphone
Chimes

Bass Clef

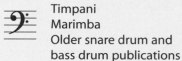

Timpani
Marimba
Older snare drum and
bass drum publications
often use the bass clef.

Time Signature

indicates how many beats per measure
and what kind of note gets one beat.

$\frac{4}{4}$ = **4 beats** per measure
= **Quarter** note gets one beat

Note Names

Each note is on a line or space of the staff.
These note names are indicated by the Clef.

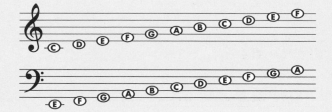

Sharp ♯ raises the note and remains in effect for the entire measure.

Flat ♭ lowers the note and remains in effect for the entire measure.

Natural ♮ cancels a flat (♭) or sharp (♯) and remains in effect for the entire measure.

Keyboard Percussion

This chart will help you play notes on orchestra bells. Practice
all exercises with other percussionists using the keyboard
percussion section at the end of this book. Switch parts often!

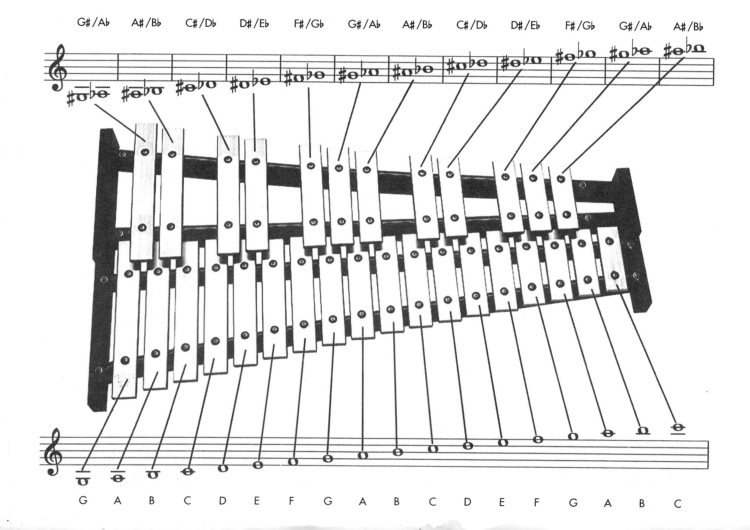

| Double Bar | indicates the end of a piece of music. | Repeat Sign | Without stopping, play once again from the beginning. |

7. THE LONG HAUL

8. FOUR BY FOUR *Practice Right Hand Lead as marked.*

Count & Tap: 1 & 2 & 3 & 4 & 1 & 2 & 3 & 4 & 1 & 2 & 3 & 4 & 1 & 2 & 3 & 4 &

9. TOUCHDOWN

10. THE FAB FIVE *Right Hand Lead*

1 & 2 & 3 & 4 & 1 & 2 & 3 & 4 & 1 & 2 & 3 & 4 & 1 & 2 & 3 & 4 &

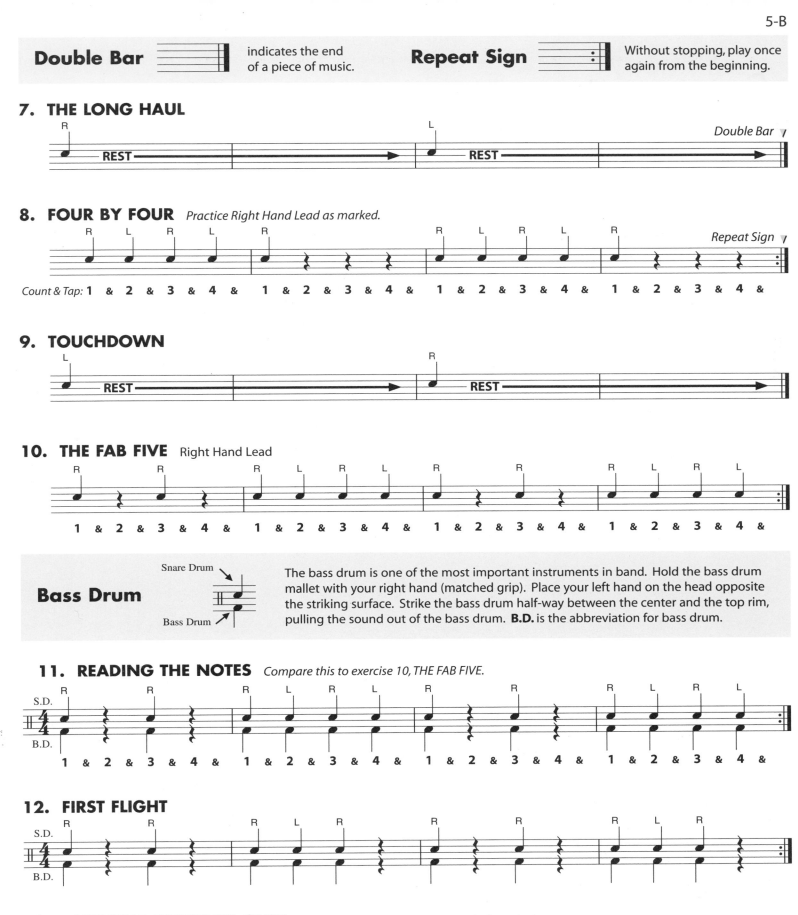

Bass Drum

The bass drum is one of the most important instruments in band. Hold the bass drum mallet with your right hand (matched grip). Place your left hand on the head opposite the striking surface. Strike the bass drum half-way between the center and the top rim, pulling the sound out of the bass drum. **B.D.** is the abbreviation for bass drum.

11. READING THE NOTES *Compare this to exercise 10, THE FAB FIVE.*

1 & 2 & 3 & 4 & 1 & 2 & 3 & 4 & 1 & 2 & 3 & 4 & 1 & 2 & 3 & 4 &

12. FIRST FLIGHT

13. ESSENTIAL ELEMENTS QUIZ *Fill in the remaining note names before playing.*

14. ROLLING ALONG

Go to the next line. ▾

Double Bar ▾

Half Note

♩ ⟶ = 2 Beats

1 & 2 &

Half Rest

= 2 Silent Beats

1 & 2 &

=

15. RHYTHM RAP *Clap the rhythm while counting and tapping.*

Clap

Repeat Sign ▾

1 & 2 & 3 & 4 &   1 & 2 & 3 & 4 &   1 & 2 & 3 & 4 &   1 & 2 & 3 & 4 &   1 & 2 & 3 & 4 &   1 & 2 & 3 & 4 &

Alternate Sticking   A hand to hand sticking pattern usually beginning with the right hand.

Bass Drum   When playing half notes, use a slower stroke to *pull* the sound out of the bass drum.

16. THE HALF COUNTS *Practice Alternate Sticking as marked.*

17. HOT CROSS BUNS

18. GO TELL AUNT RHODIE

American Folk Song

19. ESSENTIAL ELEMENTS QUIZ

Using the note names and rhythms below, draw the melody notes on the staff before playing.

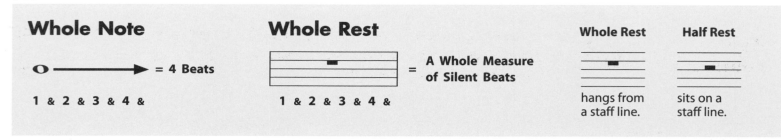

Whole Note

○ ——→ = 4 Beats

1 & 2 & 3 & 4 &

Whole Rest

= A Whole Measure of Silent Beats

1 & 2 & 3 & 4 &

Whole Rest hangs from a staff line.

Half Rest sits on a staff line.

20. RHYTHM RAP *Clap the rhythm while counting and tapping.*

Multiple Bounce

Multiple bounce sticking is your first step to learning the roll. Simply let the stick bounce freely on the drum head, like this:

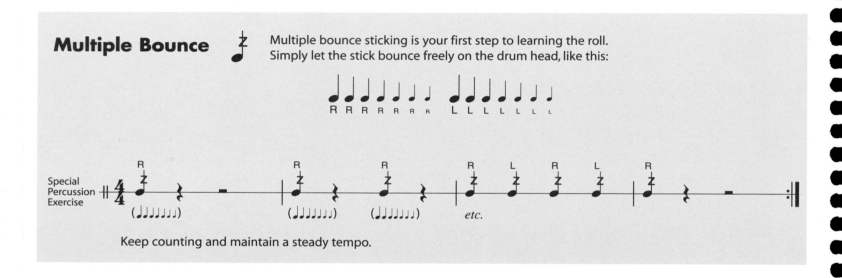

Special Percussion Exercise

Keep counting and maintain a steady tempo.

21. THE WHOLE THING *Practice this exercise with Alternate Sticking.*

Duet A composition with two different parts, played together.

Bass Drum When playing whole notes, use a very slow, long stroke to *pull* the sound out.

22. SPLIT DECISION – Duet *Play your percussion part as the brass and woodwinds play their duet parts.*

Key Signature

The **Key Signature** tells us which notes to play with sharps (♯) or flats (♭) throughout the music. When playing keyboard percussion, this key signature indicates the *Key of B♭* – play all B's as B-flats, and E's as E-flats.

23. MARCH STEPS

24. LISTEN TO OUR SECTIONS

25. LIGHTLY ROW   *Mark your own sticking before you play.*

26. ESSENTIAL ELEMENTS QUIZ   *Draw in the bar lines before you play.*

Fermata 　 Hold the note (or rest) longer than normal.

Rudiments

Rudiments are the basic techniques of playing snare drum. You should practice and memorize rudiments to improve your skill. The flam is your first rudiment.

Flam 　 The small note is a grace note. It has no rhythmic value and sounds just ahead of the regular sized, or primary note. The primary note sounds on the beat.

Right Hand Flam 　 Hold the left stick about 2 inches above the drum head. Hold the right stick in the "up" position. Move both sticks at the same speed. The left stick will hit the drum just before the right stick. Let the left stick rebound to the "up" position, and the right stick rebound to the 2 inch position.

Left Hand Flam 　 Hold the right stick about 2 inches above the drum head. Hold the left stick in the "up" position. Move both sticks at the same speed. The right stick will hit the drum just before the left stick. Let the right stick rebound to the "up" position and the left stick rebound to the 2 inch position.

A flam produces a sound that is slightly longer than a regular note (a tap).
Listen to the difference between flams and taps.

27. REACHING HIGHER

28. AU CLAIRE DE LA LUNE

French Folk Song

29. REMIX

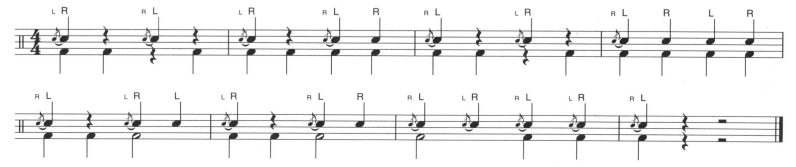

Harmony

Two or more notes played together. Each combination forms a *chord*.
Listen to the band's harmony while you play.

30. LONDON BRIDGE *Mark your own sticking before you play.*

English Folk Song

Austrian composer **Wolfgang Amadeus Mozart** (1756–1791) was a child prodigy who started playing professionally at age six, and lived during the time of the American Revolution. Mozart's music is melodic and imaginative. He wrote more than 600 compositions during his short life, including a piano piece based on the famous song, "Twinkle, Twinkle, Little Star."

Triangle

The triangle should be suspended on a clip and held at eye level. Use a metal triangle beater and hit the triangle opposite the open end. To stop the sound, touch the instrument with your fingers. **Tri.** is the abbreviation for triangle.

31. A MOZART MELODY

Adaptation

32. ESSENTIAL ELEMENTS QUIZ *Draw these symbols where they belong and write in the note names before you play:*

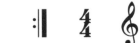

Eighth Note & Eighth Rest

Each Eighth Note or Rest = ½ Beat
2 Eighth Notes or Rests = 1 Beat

Eighth Notes groups have a *beam*.

2-note beam   4-note beam

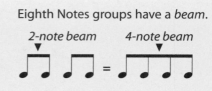

33. DEEP POCKETS

34. DOODLE ALL DAY   *Mark the sticking before you play.*

Doubling or Double Sticking

A pattern in which two consecutive notes are played with the same hand (R R L L, R R L L).
Double Sticking, or Doubling is an important skill for snare drum.

35. JUMP ROPE   *Follow the Double Sticking carefully and strive for a consistent sound.*

Pick-Up Notes

One or more notes that come before the first *full* measure. The beats of Pick-Up Notes are
subtracted from the last measure.

Rudiment
Paradiddle

A snare drum rudiment (see measure 7.)

36. A-TISKET, A-TASKET

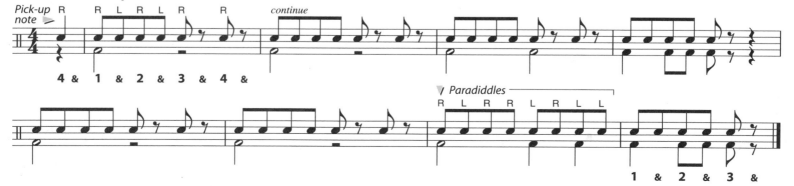

Dynamics

f – *forte* (play loudly)
lift sticks higher

mf – *mezzo forte* (play moderately loud)
normal stick height

p – *piano* (play softly)
bring sticks close to head

37. LOUD AND SOFT

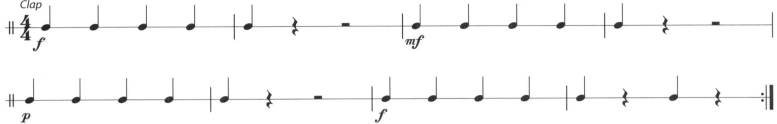

38. JINGLE BELLS

J. S. Pierpont

39. MY DREYDL *Practice "Doubling" in this exercise.*

Traditional Hanukkah Song

40. RHYTHM RAP *Clap the rhythm while counting and tapping.*

Clap

1 & 2 & 3 & 4 & 1 & 2 & 3 & 4 & 1 & 2 & 3 & 4 & 1 & 2 & 3 & 4 &

Multiple Bounce Eighth Notes

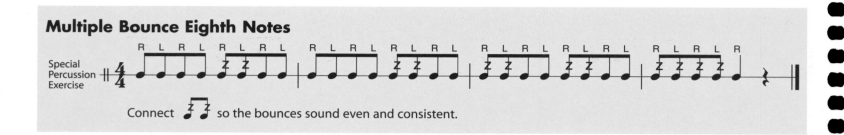

Special Percussion Exercise

Connect so the bounces sound even and consistent.

41. EIGHTH NOTE JAM

1 & 2 & 3 & 4 & 1 & 2 & 3 & 4 & 1 & 2 & 3 & 4 & 1 & 2 & 3 & 4 &

Suspended Cymbal

One single cymbal suspended on a stand. Always use yarn mallets, not timpani mallets. **Sus. Cym.** is the abbreviation for suspended cymbal.

42. SKIP TO MY LOU

American Folk Song

S.D.

B.D.

Sus. Cym.

43. LONG, LONG AGO

Wood Block

Cup your palm to form a resonating chamber under the wood block.

Curved wood block—strike on top near the center using a hard rubber mallet or snare drum stick if necessary.

Flat wood block—the best sound is toward the edge of the top surface near the side with the open slit. You should use a hard rubber mallet or wooden xylophone mallet. A drumstick does not produce a good sound on a flat wood block.

Wd. Blk. is the abbreviation for wood block.

44. OH, SUSANNA

Stephen Collins Foster

Italian composer **Gioacchino Rossini** (1792–1868) began composing as a teenager and was very proficient on the piano, viola and horn. He wrote "William Tell" at age 37 as the last of his forty operas, and its familiar theme is still heard today on radio and television.

HISTORY

Crash Cymbals

Hold the left cymbal in front of you at a slight angle. Allow the right cymbal to be positioned slightly above and slightly in front of the left cymbal.

Learn the basic stroke for a quarter note. Using a glancing stroke (and gravity), allow the right cymbal to drop into the left cymbal and follow through. This same motion is used for half notes, but slower in speed. For whole notes, the same motion is slower than for half notes.

To stop the sound of the cymbals, bring both edges of the plates against your body.

Choke = muffle (or stop) the sound immediately.

Cr. Cym. is the abbreviation for crash cymbals.

45. ESSENTIAL ELEMENTS QUIZ — WILLIAM TELL

Gioacchino Rossini

THEORY

2/4 Time Signature

= **2 beats** per measure
= **Quarter** note gets one beat

Conducting

Practice conducting this two-beat pattern.

46. RHYTHM RAP

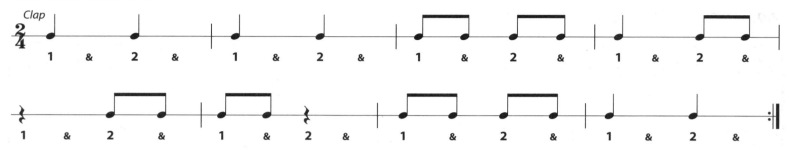

Rudiment

Flam Tap

After you play a flam, play a tap, always with the low hand. This will keep your hands correctly positioned for the rest of the exercise. Remember, a tap is played with the stick closest to the drum head.

Solo

In ensemble music, *Solo* marks a passage where one instrument takes a leading part. In the next exercise, the Bass Drum is featured in the places marked *Solo*.

47. TWO BY TWO

Be careful to maintain the same tempo when going from flam taps (measures 1 and 2) to the regular flams in measure 3.

Tempo Markings

Tempo is the speed of music. Tempo markings are usually written above the staff, in Italian.

Allegro – Fast tempo   **Moderato** – Medium tempo   **Andante** – Slower walking tempo

48. HIGH SCHOOL CADETS – March

John Philip Sousa

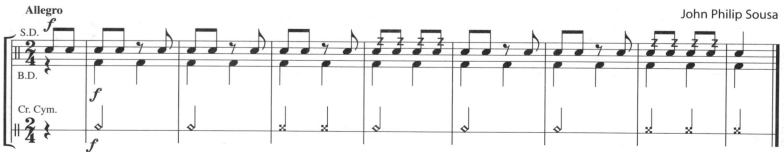

Use a slower motion on half note crashes.

Tambourine

Hold the tambourine steady in your left hand at a slight upward angle.
Your right hand strikes the head of the instrument according to the written dynamics:

Soft light sounds use one or two fingertips near the edge of the head.
Medium loud sounds use tips of all fingers one-third of the way from the edge to the center.
Loud sounds knuckles on head, half-way between edge and the center.
Use a motion similar to knocking on a door.

49. HEY, HO! NOBODY'S HOME

Dynamics

Crescendo (gradually louder)   *Decrescendo* or *Diminuendo* (gradually softer)

50. CLAP THE DYNAMICS

Suspended Cymbal Roll

With yarn mallets on a suspended cymbal, use a rapid series of alternate strokes on the opposite edges of the cymbal (3 o'clock and 9 o'clock). Increase the speed of the roll to build an effective crescendo.

51. PLAY THE DYNAMICS

PERFORMANCE SPOTLIGHT

52. PERFORMANCE WARM-UPS

TONE BUILDER

RHYTHM ETUDE

RHYTHM RAP

Remember: how your hand strikes the tambourine is determined by the dynamics.

Let Ring ♩⌢ = Let the sound continue to "ring" without stopping. It is a common indication for triangle or cymbals. The same effect is sometimes marked *l.v.* (let vibrate) or *l.r.* (let ring).

CHORALE

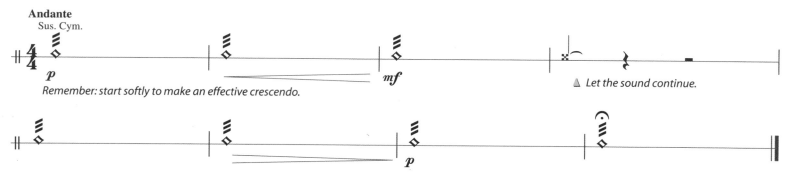

Remember: start softly to make an effective crescendo.

Triangle

Striking the side opposite the open end will produce a "fundamental" sound.
Striking the bottom leg will produce a sound with more overtones (ringing).
Listen to the band and decide which sound works best with music. It's your choice!

53. AURA LEE – Duet or Band Arrangement

George R. Poulton

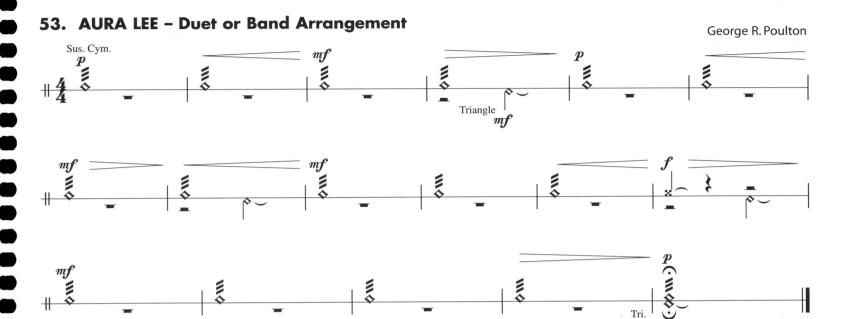

54. FRÈRE JACQUES – Round *(When group A reaches ②, group B begins at ①)*

French Folk Song

PERFORMANCE SPOTLIGHT

55. WHEN THE SAINTS GO MARCHING IN – Band Arrangement

Arr. by John Higgins

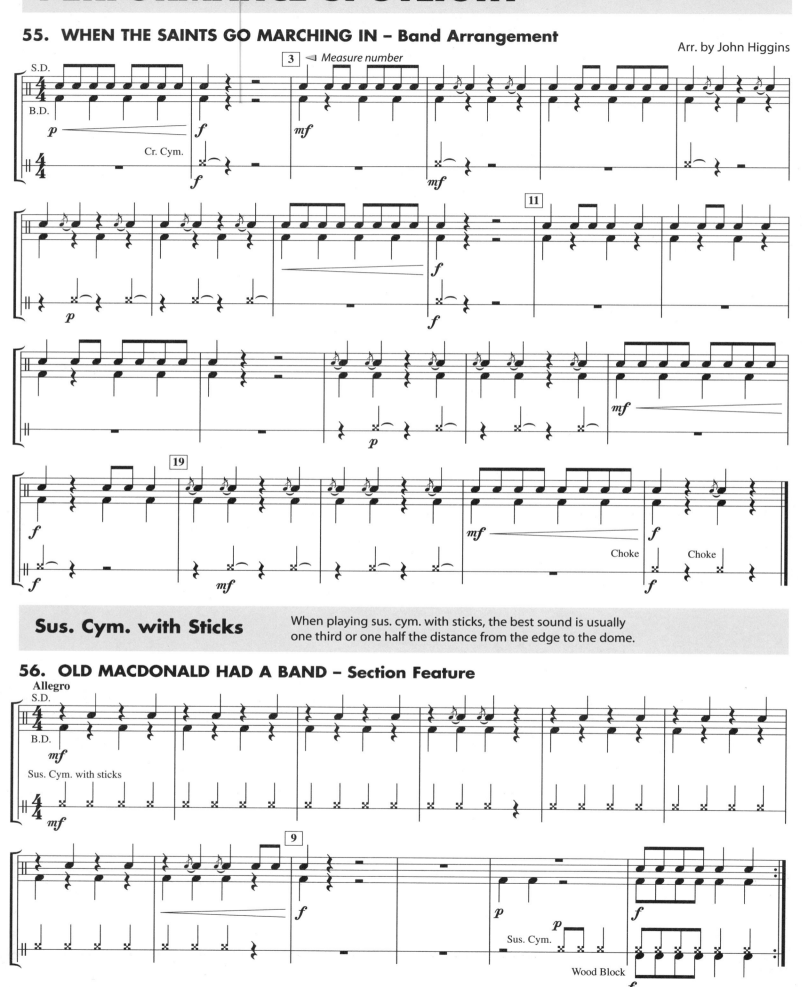

Sus. Cym. with Sticks

When playing sus. cym. with sticks, the best sound is usually one third or one half the distance from the edge to the dome.

56. OLD MACDONALD HAD A BAND – Section Feature

After repeating, go on to next page

57. ODE TO JOY (from Symphony No. 9)

Ludwig van Beethoven
Arr. by John Higgins

58. HARD ROCK BLUES – Encore

John Higgins

Tie

Pitched Percussion
(Keyboards and Timpani)

 = 2 Beats

A curved line connecting notes of the same pitch.
Play one note for the combined counts of the tied notes.

Other Percussion
(S.D., B.D., Tamb., Cym., etc.)

= 2 Beats

A curved line connecting two notes on the same staff line or space. Play one note for the combined counts of the tied notes.

59. FIT TO BE TIED

60. ALOUETTE

French-Canadian Folk Song

Dotted Half Note

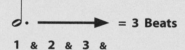 = 3 Beats

1 & 2 & 3 &

 Dot

A dot adds half the value of the note.

 =

2 beats + 1 beat = 3 beats

61. ALOUETTE – THE SEQUEL

French-Canadian Folk Song

HISTORY

American composer **Stephen Collins Foster** (1826–1864) was born near Pittsburgh, PA. He has become the most recognized song writer of his time for works such as "Oh Susanna," which became popular during the California Gold Rush of 1849. Among his most well-known songs are "My Old Kentucky Home" and "Camptown Races."

62. CAMPTOWN RACES   *Practice Flam Taps in this exercise.*

Stephen Collins Foster

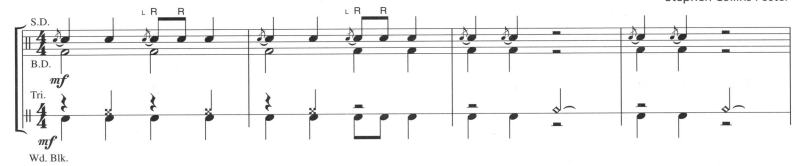

63. NEW DIRECTIONS

64. THE NOBLES

65. ESSENTIAL ELEMENTS QUIZ

THEORY

¾ Time Signature

= **3 beats** per measure
= **Quarter** note gets one beat

Conducting

Practice conducting this three-beat pattern.

66. RHYTHM RAP

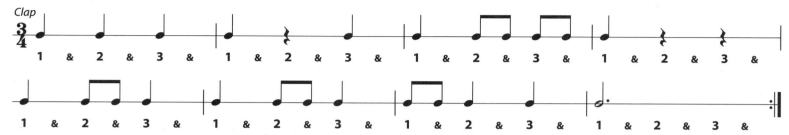

Clap

1 & 2 & 3 & 1 & 2 & 3 & 1 & 2 & 3 & 1 & 2 & 3 &

1 & 2 & 3 & 1 & 2 & 3 & 1 & 2 & 3 & 1 & 2 & 3 &

Rudiment

Double Paradiddle

67. THREE BEAT JAM

68. BARCAROLLE

Jacques Offenbach

Moderato

mf

HISTORY

Norwegian composer **Edvard Grieg** (1843–1907) wrote *Peer Gynt Suite* for a play by Henrik Ibsen in 1875, the year before the telephone was invented by Alexander Graham Bell. "Morning" is a melody from *Peer Gynt Suite*. Music used in plays, or in films and television, is called **incidental music**.

Rudiment

Flam Accent

After you play a flam, play two strokes, always with the high hand. This will keep your hands properly positioned.

69. MORNING (from Peer Gynt)

Andante

Edvard Grieg

S.D.

B.D.

p

Tri.

p

mf

p

mf

p

Accent

♩ > Emphasize the note.

70. ACCENT YOUR TALENT

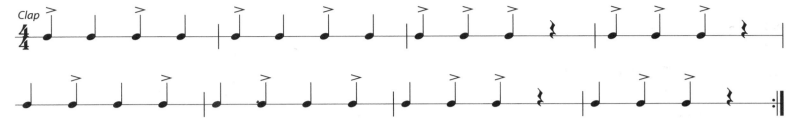

HISTORY

Latin American music has its roots in the African, Native American, Spanish and Portuguese cultures. This diverse music features lively accompaniments by drums and other percussion instruments such as maracas and claves. Music from Latin America continues to influence jazz, classical and popular styles of music. "Chiapanecas" is a popular children's dance and game song.

Maracas
Hold maracas by the handles. Use a short, precise wrist motion to shake maracas. Maintain a steady tempo.

Claves
Cup your left hand to form a resonating chamber. Hold the lower pitched clave in your left hand. Use the clave in your right hand to strike the center of the left clave.

Rim Shot
R.S.

Place tip of left stick on center of drum. Rest stick on rim and hold firmly. Strike with right stick about 1/3 away from tip of left stick. **R.S.** is the abbreviation for rim shot.

71. MEXICAN CLAPPING SONG ("Chiapanecas")

Latin American Folk Song

72. ESSENTIAL CREATIVITY

Compose your own melody for measures 3 and 4 using this rhythm:

This percussion part can be played to accompany a band member's melody.

73. HOT MUFFINS

74. COSSACK DANCE

75. BASIC BLUES

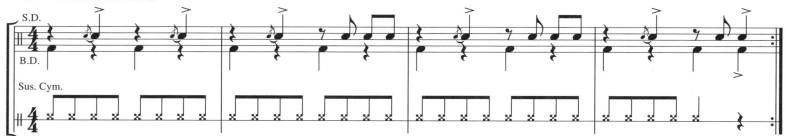

 THEORY

Key Signature

The **Key Signature** tells us which notes to play with sharps or flats throughout the music. For keyboard percussion, this Key Signature indicates the *Key of F* – play all B's as B-flats.

1st & 2nd Endings

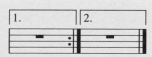

Play through the 1st Ending. Then play the repeated section of music, **skipping** the 1st Ending and playing the 2nd Ending.

76. HIGH FLYING

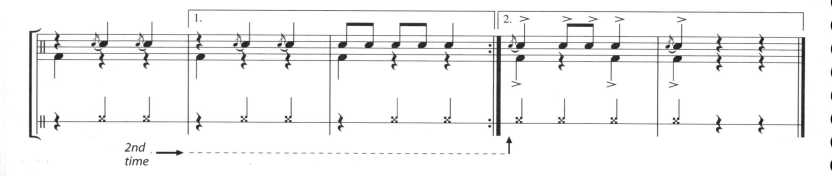

2nd time →

Japanese folk music actually has its origins in ancient China. "Sakura, Sakura" was performed on instruments such as the **koto**, a 13-string instrument that is more than 4000 years old, and the **shakuhachi** or bamboo flute. The unique sound of this ancient Japanese melody results from the pentatonic (or five-note) sequence used in this tonal system.

Snare Drum — Turning the snares off can create an effective, dark sound, similar to a tom-tom.

77. SAKURA, SAKURA – Band Arrangement

Japanese Folk Song
Arr. by John Higgins

S.D. and B.D. can share the same rest.

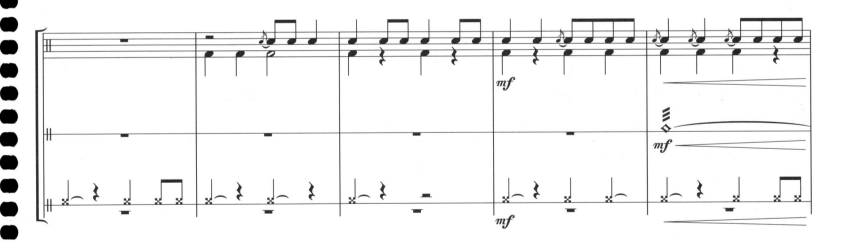

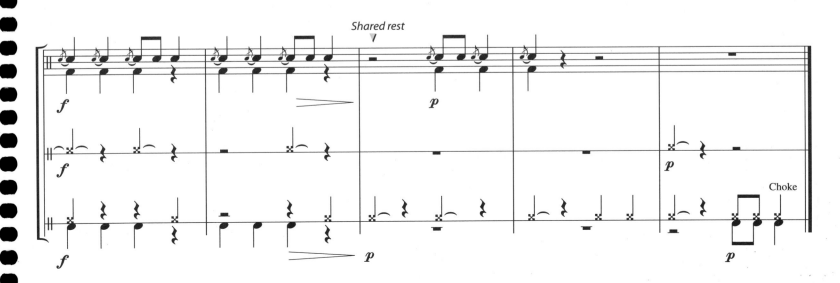

17-A

Sleigh Bells

Sleigh bells are usually shaken on the rhythm indicated. However, handle-mounted sleigh bells can be tapped gently in time with the fist by holding the instrument perpendicular to the floor.

78. UP ON A HOUSETOP

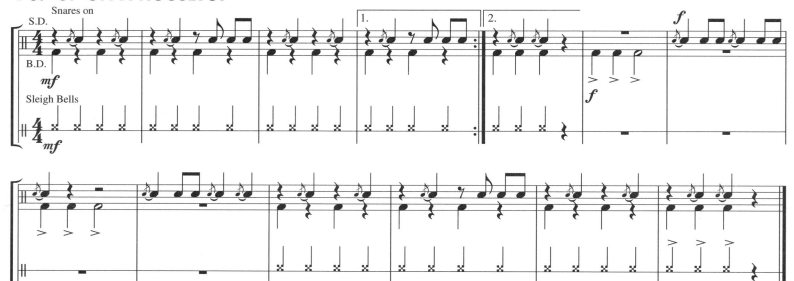

79. JOLLY OLD ST. NICK   *Remember to emphasize the accented notes.*

80. THE BIG AIRSTREAM

81. WALTZ THEME (THE MERRY WIDOW WALTZ)

Franz Lehar

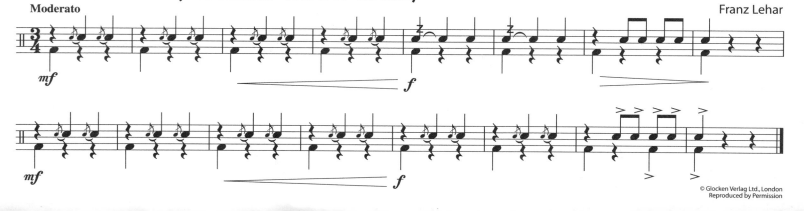

Sixteenth Notes

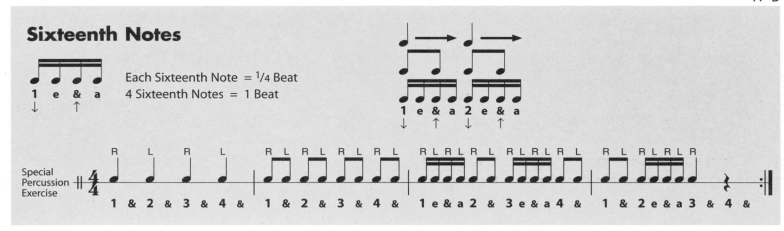

Each Sixteenth Note = 1/4 Beat
4 Sixteenth Notes = 1 Beat

Special Percussion Exercise

82. AIR TIME *Count carefully and maintain a steady tempo.*

83. DOWN BY THE STATION

84. ESSENTIAL ELEMENTS QUIZ

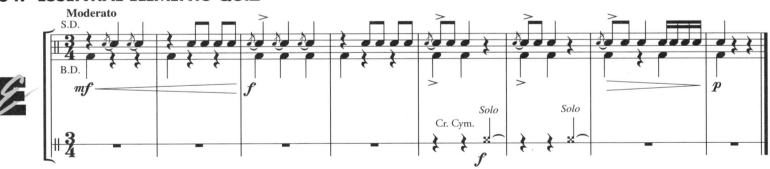

85. ESSENTIAL CREATIVITY *Improvise your own part for measures 3–8 using these rhythms:* ♩, ♫, ♬

DAILY WARM-UPS

WORK-OUTS FOR TONE & TECHNIQUE

86. TONE BUILDER

87. RHYTHM BUILDER

88. TECHNIQUE TRAX

89. CHORALE *(Adapted from Cantata 147)*

Johann Sebastian Bach

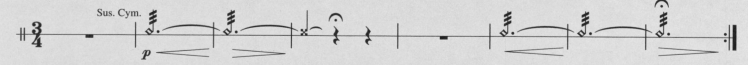

THEORY

Theme and Variations

A musical form featuring a **theme**, or primary melody, followed by **variations**, or altered versions of the theme.

90. VARIATIONS ON A FAMILIAR THEME

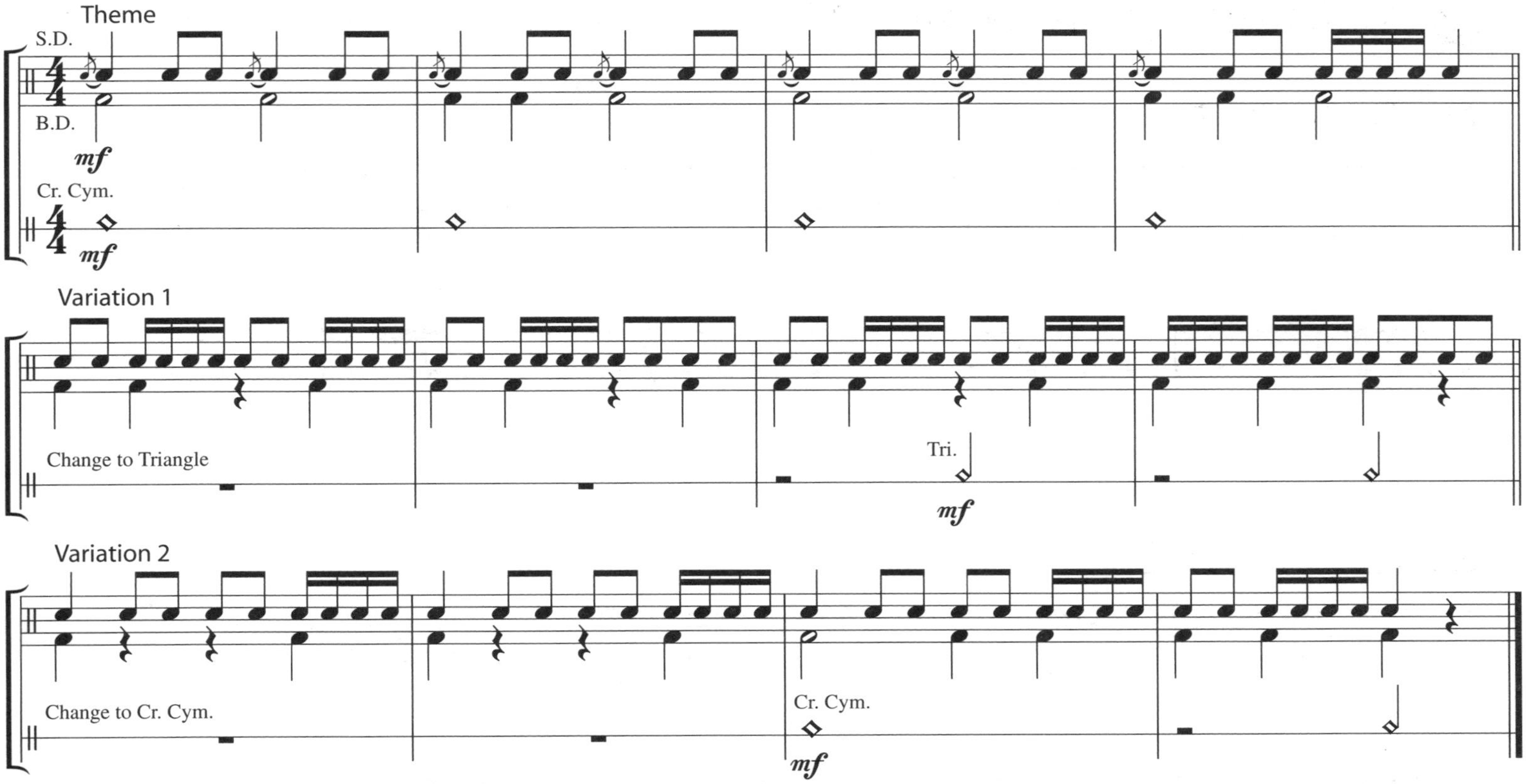

Theme
S.D.
B.D.
mf
Cr. Cym.
mf
Variation 1
Change to Triangle
Tri.
mf
Variation 2
Change to Cr. Cym.
Cr. Cym.
mf

D.C. al Fine

At the **D.C. al Fine** play again from the beginning, stopping at **Fine** *(fee'- nay)*.
D.C. is the abbreviation for **Da Capo**, or "to the beginning," and **Fine** means "the end."

Eighth Note Two Sixteenths

1 e & a

= 1 Beat
Subdivide each beat into 4 equal parts.

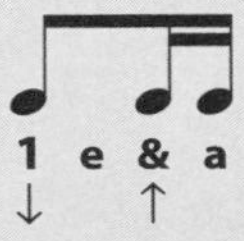

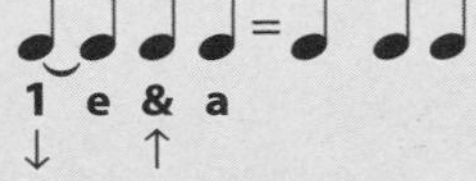

1 e & a

1 e & a 2 e & a

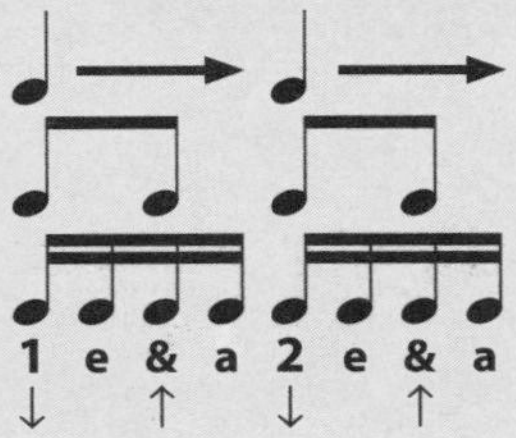

91. BANANA BOAT SONG

Caribbean Folk Song

Moderato
Snares off
S.D.
B.D.
f
Maracas
f
Fine
mf
mf
mf
D.C. al Fine

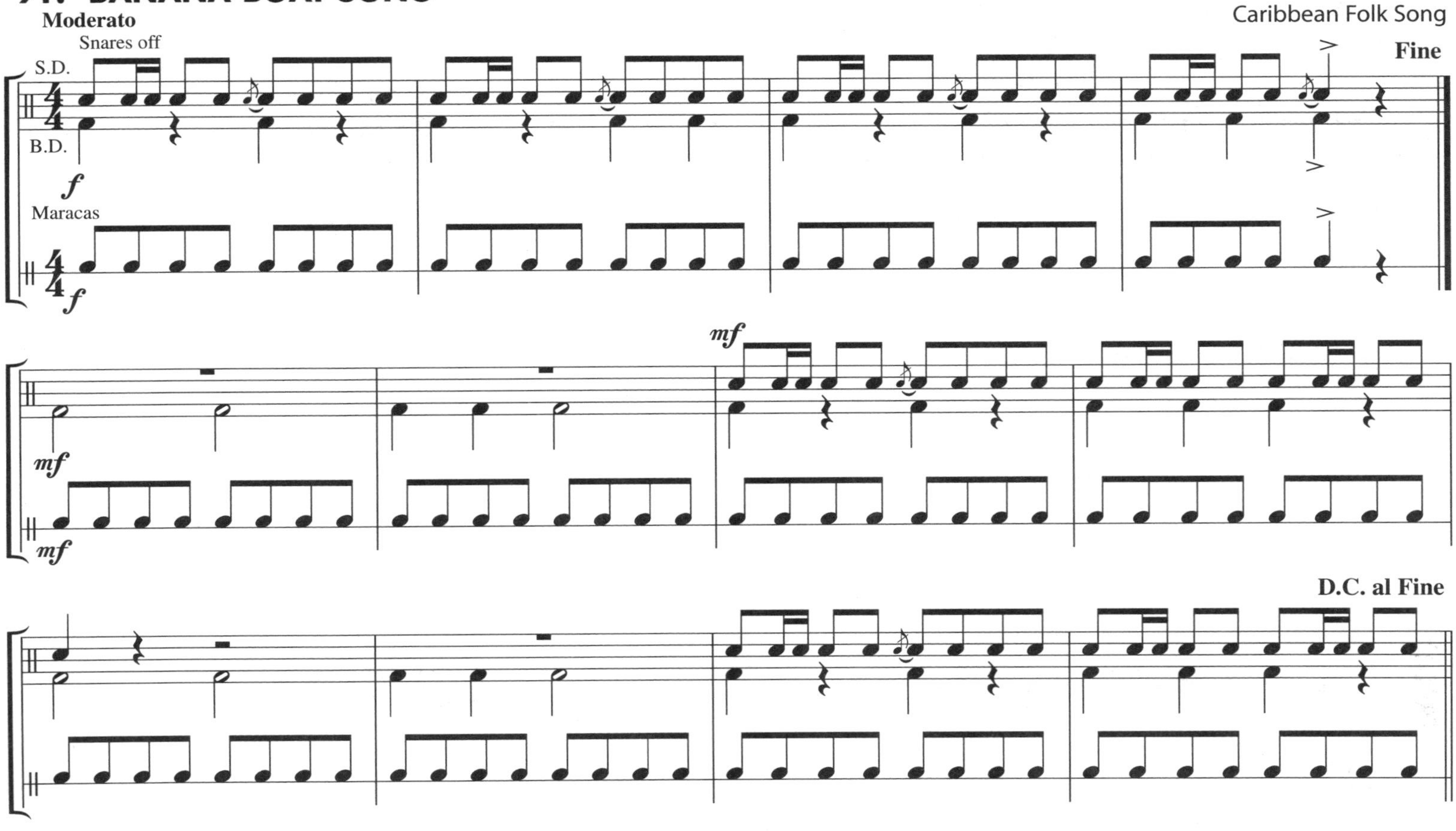

92. RAZOR'S EDGE

Snares on

93. THE MUSIC BOX

HISTORY

African-American spirituals originated in the 1700's, midway through the period of slavery in the United States. One of the largest categories of true American folk music, these primarily religious songs were sung and passed on for generations without being written down. The first collection of spirituals was published in 1867, four years after The Emancipation Proclamation was signed into law.

---

94. EZEKIEL SAW THE WHEEL

African-American Spiritual

Allegro

95. SMOOTH OPERATOR

Rim Shot

▼ *Note how the pattern changed.*

96. GLIDING ALONG *Practice "Doubling" in this exercise.*

Ragtime is an American music style that was popular from the 1890's until the time of World War I. This early form of jazz brought fame to pianists like "Jelly Roll" Morton and Scott Joplin, who wrote "The Entertainer" and "Maple Leaf Rag." Surprisingly, the style was incorporated into some orchestral music by Igor Stravinsky and Claude Debussy. The trombones now learn to play a *glissando*, a technique used in ragtime and other styles of music.

HISTORY

97. TROMBONE RAG

98. ESSENTIAL ELEMENTS QUIZ

99. TAKE THE LEAD *Practice Right Hand Lead in this exercise.*

THEORY

Phrase

A musical "sentence" which is often 2 or 4 measures long. Percussionists should match the dynamics of the band.

---

100. THE COLD WIND

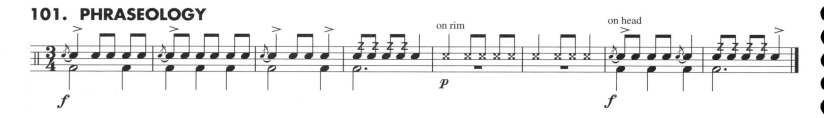

---

101. PHRASEOLOGY

THEORY

Multiple Measure Rest

The number above the staff tells you how many full measures to rest. Count each measure of rest in sequence:

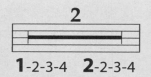

1-2-3-4 **2**-2-3-4

Simile (*sim.*)

Continue playing in the same style.

---

102. SATIN LATIN *Practice Double Sticking in this exercise.*

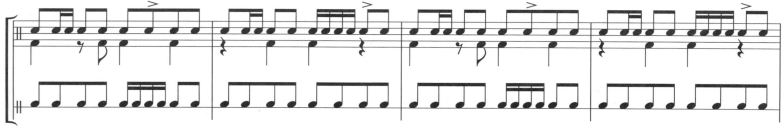

German composer **Johann Sebastian Bach** (1685–1750) was part of a large family of famous musicians and became the most recognized composer of the Baroque era. Beginning as a choir member, Bach soon became an organist, a teacher, and a prolific composer, writing more than 600 masterworks. This *Minuet,* or dance in 3/4 time, was written as a teaching piece for use with an early form of the piano.

HISTORY

103. MINUET

Moderato

Johann Sebastian Bach

Snares on

104. ESSENTIAL CREATIVITY

This melody can be played in 3/4 or 4/4. Pencil in either time signature, draw the bar lines and play. Now erase the bar lines and try the other time signature. Do the phrases sound different?

105. NATURALLY Right Hand Lead

HISTORY

Austrian composer **Franz Peter Schubert** (1797–1828) lived a shorter life than any other great composer, but he created an incredible amount of music: more than 600 art-songs (concert music for voice and accompaniment), ten symphonies, chamber music, operas, choral works and piano pieces. His "March Militaire" was originally a piano duet.

THEORY

One Measure Repeat   Repeat the previous measure.

106. MARCH MILITAIRE *Practice "Doubling" in this exercise.*

Franz Schubert

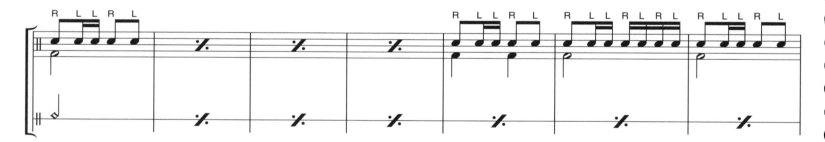

107. THE FLAT ZONE

108. ON TOP OF OLD SMOKEY

American Folk Song

Boogie-woogie is a style of the **blues**, and it was first recorded by pianist Clarence "Pine Top" Smith in 1928, one year after Charles Lindbergh's solo flight across the Atlantic. A form of jazz, blues music features altered notes and is usually written in 12-measure verses, like "Bottom Bass Boogie."

HISTORY

109. BOTTOM BASS BOOGIE

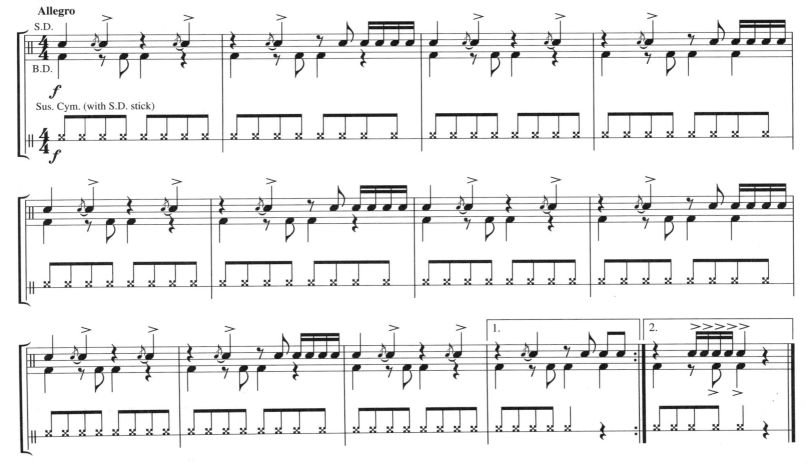

Dotted Quarter & Eighth Notes

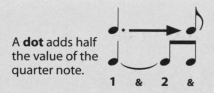

A **dot** adds half the value of the quarter note.

110. RHYTHM RAP

111. THE DOT ALWAYS COUNTS

Closed Roll

Subdivide each ♩ into 4 equal strokes, and connect the multiple bounces as smoothly as possible. Closed rolls fill each beat with a buzzing sound.

112. ALL THROUGH THE NIGHT

113. SEA CHANTY

English Folk Song

114. SCARBOROUGH FAIR

English Folk Song

115. RHYTHM RAP

116. THE TURNAROUND

117. ESSENTIAL ELEMENTS QUIZ – AULD LANG SYNE

Scottish Folk Song

PERFORMANCE SPOTLIGHT

Solo with Piano Accompaniment

You can perform this snare drum solo with a piano accompaniment. Play it for the band, the school or your family. The theme in the piano part is a well-known melody from a set of orchestral works called **Hungarian Dances**, by the German composer **Johannes Brahms** (1833–1897). Many of Brahms' works include dance and folk styles he learned from touring Europe as a young man.

118. HUNGARIAN DANCE NO. 5 – Snare Drum Solo

Johannes Brahms
Arr. by Will Rapp

*Hit sticks together.

118. HUNGARIAN DANCE NO. 5 – Piano Accompaniment

Johannes Brahms
Arr. by Will Rapp

Great musicians give encouragement to fellow performers. On this page, clarinetists learn their instruments' upper register in the "Grenadilla Gorilla Jumps" (named after the grenadilla wood used to make clarinets). Brass players learn lip slurs, a new warm-up pattern and percussionists combine new sticking patterns. The success of your band depends on everyone's effort and encouragement.

Snare Drum

The following exercises will help you develop important skills.
Follow the written sticking very carefully to help build your snare drum technique.

119. GRENADILLA GORILLA JUMP No. 1

120. JUMPIN' UP AND DOWN

121. GRENADILLA GORILLA JUMP No. 2

122. JUMPIN' FOR JOY

123. GRENADILLA GORILLA JUMP No. 3

124. JUMPIN' JACKS

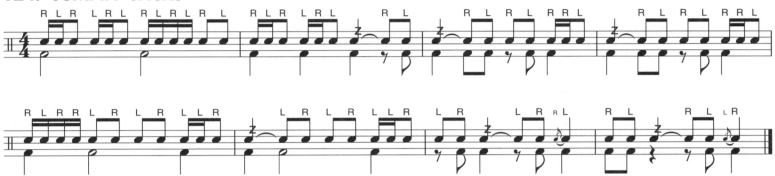

Interval

The distance between two pitches is an **interval**. Starting with "1" on the lower note, count each line and space between the notes. The number of the higher note is the distance of the interval.

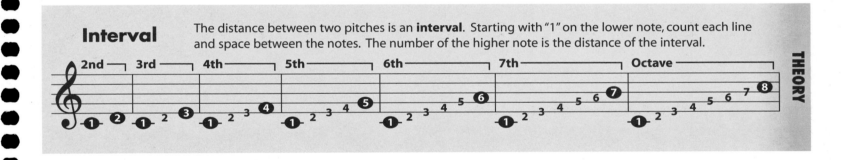

2nd 3rd 4th 5th 6th 7th Octave

THEORY

125. ESSENTIAL ELEMENTS QUIZ   *A quiz on intervals appears in the keyboard section (page 24).*

126. GRENADILLA GORILLA JUMP No. 4 *Practice Alternate Sticking as marked.*

127. THREE IS THE COUNT

128. GRENADILLA GORILLA JUMP No. 5

Closed Roll  Subdivide each  into 2 equal strokes, and connect the multiple bounces as smoothly as possible.

129. TECHNIQUE TRAX

130. CROSSING OVER

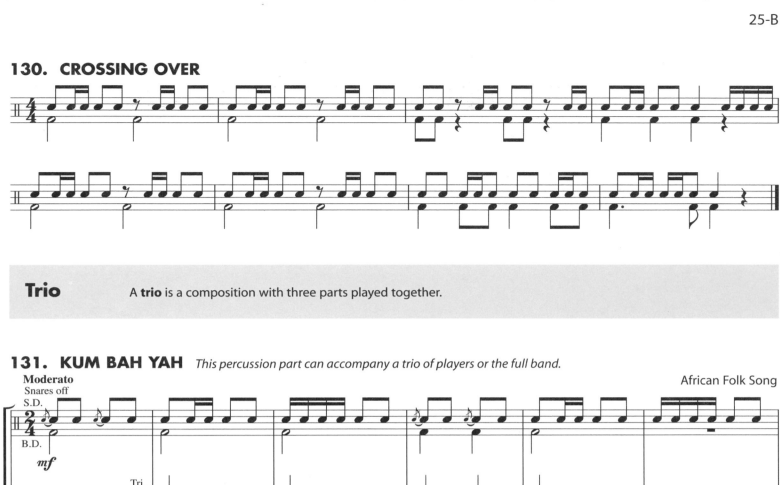

Trio

A **trio** is a composition with three parts played together.

131. KUM BAH YAH

This percussion part can accompany a trio of players or the full band.

African Folk Song

Repeat Signs

Repeat the section of music enclosed by the **repeat signs**.
(If 1st and 2nd endings are used, they are played as usual — but go back only to the first repeat sign, not to the beginning.)

132. MICHAEL ROW THE BOAT ASHORE
Flam accents can also apply to eighth notes.

African-American Spiritual

133. AUSTRIAN WALTZ

Austrian Folk Song

134. BOTANY BAY

Australian Folk Song

THEORY

 **Time Signature**

 = **Common Time**
(Same as $\frac{4}{4}$)

Conducting

Practice conducting
this four-beat pattern.

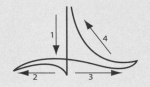

135. TECHNIQUE TRAX *Practice at all dynamic levels.*

136. FINLANDIA

Jean Sibelius

137. ESSENTIAL CREATIVITY

Create your own variations by penciling in a dot and a flag to change the rhythm of any measure from

138. EASY GORILLA JUMPS

139. TECHNIQUE TRAX

140. MORE TECHNIQUE TRAX

141. GERMAN FOLK SONG

142. THE SAINTS GO MARCHIN' AGAIN

James Black and Katherine Purvis

143. LOWLAND GORILLA WALK

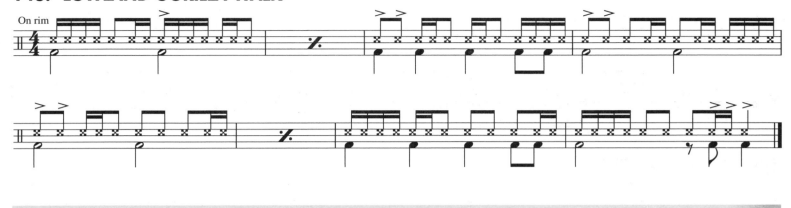

Two Measure Repeat

Repeat the previous two measures.

144. SMOOTH SAILING

145. MORE GORILLA JUMPS

146. FULL COVERAGE

28-A

THEORY

Scale

A **scale** is a sequence of notes in ascending or descending order. Like a musical "ladder," each step is the next consecutive note in the key. See exercise 147 in the keyboard section.

Extended Roll

Subdivide each beat into 4 equal strokes and connect the multiple bounces as smoothly as possible. Extended rolls are closed rolls which fill all beats with a buzzing sound.

147. CONCERT B♭ SCALE

THEORY

Chord & Arpeggio

When two or more notes are played together, they form a **chord** or **harmony**. See exercise 148 in the keyboard section.

148. IN HARMONY

149. SCALE AND ARPEGGIO

Austrian composer **Franz Josef Haydn** (1732–1809) wrote 104 symphonies. Many of these works had nicknames and included brilliant, unique effects for their time. His Symphony No. 94 was named "The Surprise Symphony" because the soft second movement included a sudden loud dynamic, intended to wake up an often sleepy audience. Pay special attention to dynamics when you play this famous theme.

150. THEME FROM "SURPRISE SYMPHONY"

Franz Josef Haydn

151. ESSENTIAL ELEMENTS QUIZ – THE STREETS OF LAREDO

American Folk Song

PERFORMANCE SPOTLIGHT

152. SCHOOL SPIRIT – Band Arrangement

W.T. Purdy
Arr. by John Higgins

Soli

When playing music marked **Soli**, you are part of a group "solo" or group feature. Listen carefully in "Carnival of Venice," and name the instruments that play the Soli part at each indicated measure number.

153. CARNIVAL OF VENICE – Band Arrangement

Julius Benedict
Arr. by John Higgins

*In some printed music, cymbals appear with the bass drum.

DAILY WARM-UPS

WORK-OUTS FOR TONE & TECHNIQUE

154. RANGE AND FLEXIBILITY BUILDER

Rudiment

Triple Paradiddle

155. TECHNIQUE TRAX *Emphasize the accents.*

156. CHORALE

Johann Sebastian Bach

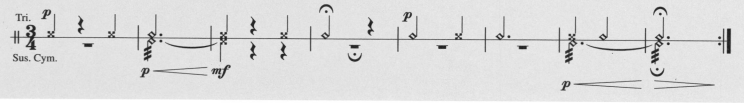

HISTORY

The traditional Hebrew melody "Hatikvah" has been Israel's national anthem since the nation's inception. At the Declaration of State in 1948, it was sung by the gathered assembly during the opening ceremony and played by members of the Palestine Symphony Orchestra at its conclusion.

157. HATIKVAH

Israeli National Anthem

158. RHYTHM RAP

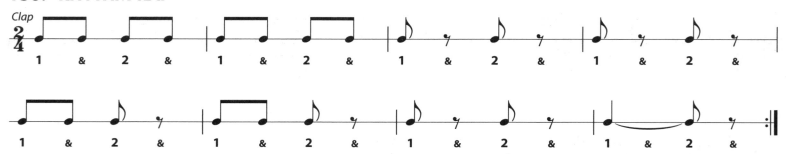

159. EIGHTH NOTE MARCH *Practice "Doubling" and Paradiddles.*

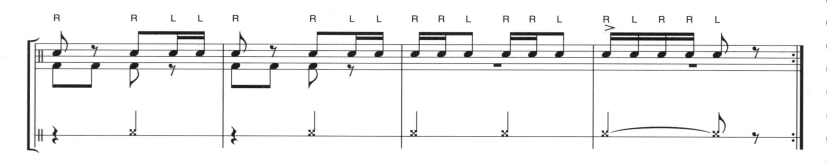

160. MINUET

Johann Sebastian Bach

161. RHYTHM RAP

162. EIGHT NOTES OFF THE BEAT

Cowbell   Hold the open end of the cowbell away from you,
and play on the front edge of the open end with a stick.

163. EIGHTH NOTE SCRAMBLE

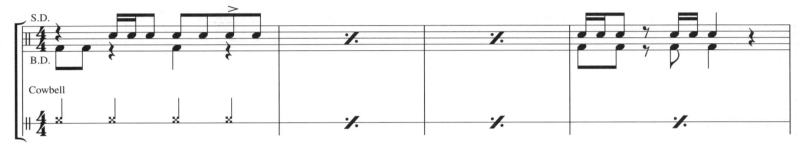

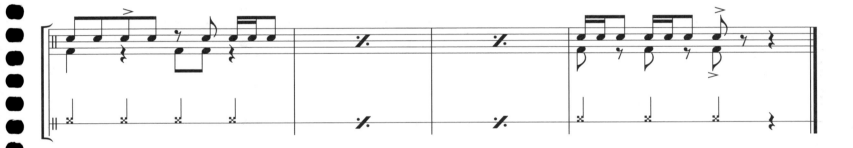

164. ESSENTIAL ELEMENTS QUIZ

165. DANCING MELODY

American composer and conductor **John Philip Sousa** (1854–1932) wrote 136 marches. Known as "The March King," Sousa wrote *The Stars And Stripes Forever, Semper Fidelis, The Washington Post* and many other patriotic works. Sousa's band performed all over the country, and his fame helped boost the popularity of bands in America. Here is a melody from his famous *El Capitan* operetta and march.

166. EL CAPITAN

John Philip Sousa

"O Canada," formerly known as the "National Song," was first performed during 1880 in French Canada. Robert Stanley Weir translated the English language version in 1908, but it was not adopted as the national anthem of Canada until 1980, one hundred years after its premiere.

167. O CANADA

Maestoso (Majestically)

Calixa Lavallee,
l'Hon. Judge Routhier
and Justice R.S. Weir

168. ESSENTIAL ELEMENTS QUIZ – METER MANIA *Count and clap before playing. Can you conduct this?*

THEORY

Enharmonics

Two notes that are written differently, but sound the same (and played with the same fingering) are called **enharmonics**. Your note chart on page 5-A shows the enharmonic notes for keyboard percussion instruments.

On a piano keyboard, each black key is both a flat and a sharp:

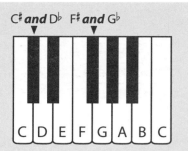

169. SNAKE CHARMER

170. DARK SHADOWS

171. CLOSE ENCOUNTERS

172. MARCH SLAV
Snare Drum is *tacet* (do not play). An optional timpani part appears on page 33-B.

Peter Illyich Tchaikovsky

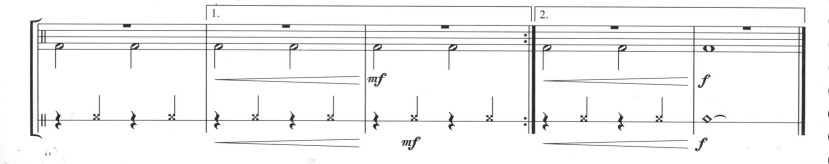

Timpani

One of the most dramatic instruments in the percussion section, *Timpani* combines the rhythms of percussion with the pitch of other instruments. Use felt timpani mallets. For **March Slav** tune the larger drum to F and the smaller drum to B♭.

172. MARCH SLAV – Timpani

Tune to F and B♭.

Largo

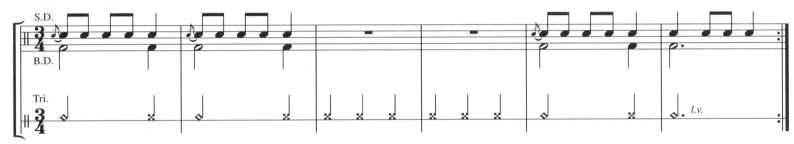

173. NOTES IN DISGUISE

Chromatic Notes

Chromatic notes are altered with sharps, flats and natural signs which are not in the key signature. The smallest distance between two notes is a half-step, and a scale made up of consecutive half-steps is called a **chromatic scale**.

THEORY

174. HALF-STEPPIN'

HISTORY

French composer **Camille Saint-Saëns** (1835–1921) wrote music for virtually every medium: operas, suites, symphonies and chamber works. The "Egyptian Dance" is one of the main themes from his famous opera *Samson et Delilah*. The opera was written in the same year that Thomas Edison invented the phonograph—1877.

Tambourine Shake Shake the tambourine in your left hand. Stop the shake on the release (tied) note with the fist of your right hand.

175. EGYPTIAN DANCE.

Camille Saint-Saëns

175. EGYPTIAN DANCE – Timpani

Tune the larger drum to A and the smaller drum to E. Watch for accidentals.
Use a light stroke to achieve a dance-like quality in your sound.

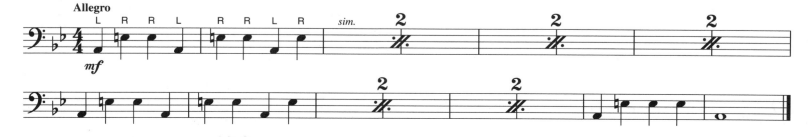

176. SILVER MOON BOAT

Chinese Folk Song

German composer **Ludwig van Beethoven** (1770–1827) is considered to be one of the world's greatest composers, despite becoming completely deaf in 1802. Although he could not hear his music the way we can, he could "hear" it in his mind. As a testament to his greatness, his Symphony No. 9 (p. 13) was performed as the finale to the ceremony celebrating the reunification of Germany in 1990. This is the theme from his Symphony No. 7, second movement.

HISTORY

177. THEME FROM SYMPHONY NO. 7

While this part looks easy, it is difficult because it is slow. Strive for an even consistent sound.

Ludwig van Beethoven

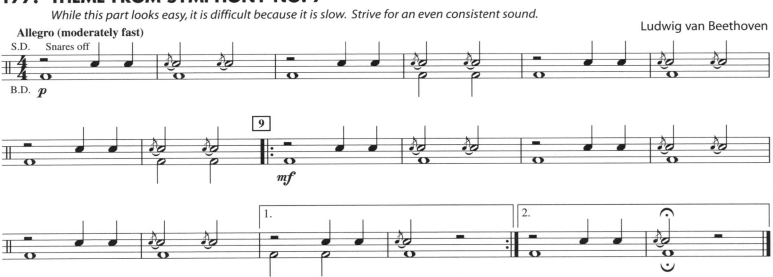

177. THEME FROM SYMPHONY NO. 7 – Timpani

Ludwig van Beethoven

Tune to E♭ and A♭.

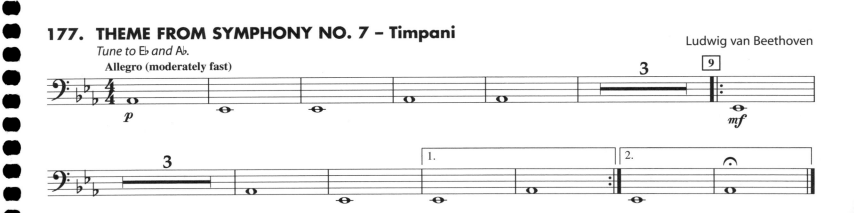

HISTORY

Russian composer **Peter Illyich Tchaikovsky** (1840–1893) wrote six symphonies and hundreds of other works including *The Nutcracker* ballet. He was a master at writing brilliant settings of folk music, and his original melodies are among the most popular of all time. His *1812 Overture* and *Capriccio Italien* were both written in 1880, the year after Thomas Edison developed the practical electric light bulb.

178. CAPRICCIO ITALIEN

Peter Illyich Tchaikovsky

178. CAPRICCIO ITALIEN – Timpani

Use a slow stroke to "pull" the sound out of the timpani. Tune to F and B♭.

Peter Illyich Tchaikovsky

Rudiment

Flamacue

A snare drum rudiment. Emphasize the ♪

179. AMERICAN PATROL

F.W. Meacham

Go on to next page

180. WAYFARING STRANGER

African-American Spiritual

181. ESSENTIAL ELEMENTS QUIZ – RUDIMENT COUNTING CONQUEST

PERFORMANCE SPOTLIGHT

182. AMERICA THE BEAUTIFUL – Band Arrangement

Samuel A. Ward
Arr. by John Higgins

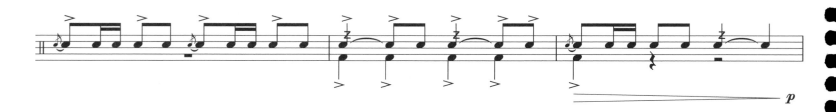

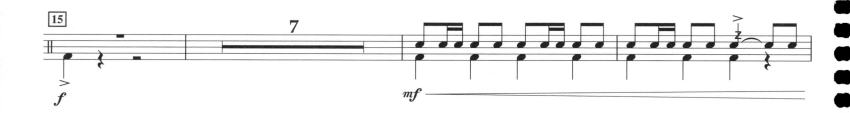

PERFORMANCE SPOTLIGHT

182. AMERICA THE BEAUTIFUL – Band Arrangement

Samuel A. Ward
Arr. by John Higgins

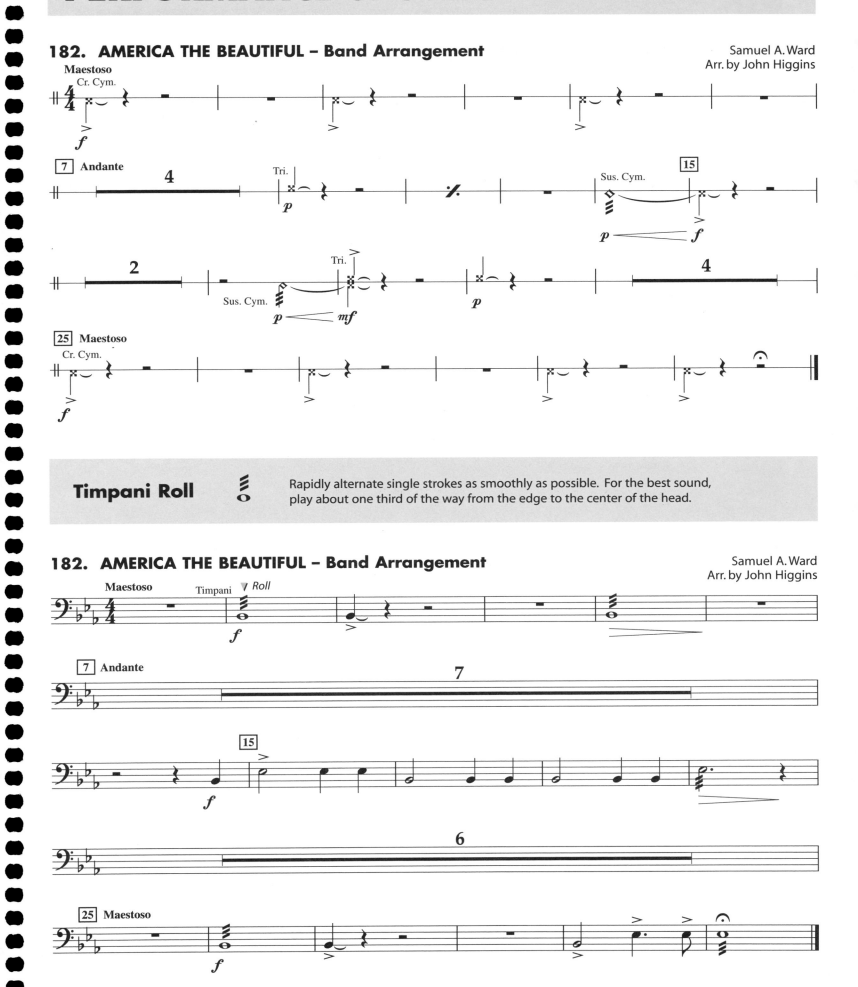

Timpani Roll — Rapidly alternate single strokes as smoothly as possible. For the best sound, play about one third of the way from the edge to the center of the head.

182. AMERICA THE BEAUTIFUL – Band Arrangement

Samuel A. Ward
Arr. by John Higgins

183. LA CUCARACHA – Band Arrangement

Latin American Folk Song
Arr. by John Higgins

183. LA CUCARACHA – Band Arrangement

Latin American Folk Song
Arr. by John Higgins

PERFORMANCE SPOTLIGHT

184. THEME FROM 1812 OVERTURE – Band Arrangement

Peter Illyich Tchaikovsky
Arr. by John Higgins

PERFORMANCE SPOTLIGHT

184. THEME FROM 1812 OVERTURE – Band Arrangement

Peter Illyich Tchaikovsky
Arr. by John Higgins

184. THEME FROM 1812 OVERTURE – Band Arrangement

Peter Illyich Tchaikovsky
Arr. by John Higgins

*Stop sound with fingertips.

PERFORMANCE SPOTLIGHT

Solo for Percussion Ensemble

Performing for an audience is an exciting part of being involved in music. Percussion ensembles provide a unique solo performing opportunity for all members of the percussion section. This percussion ensemble is written for 5 or more players. It is based on the famous "Can-Can" dance from Jacques Offenbach's operetta *Orpheus in the Underworld,* completed in 1858. Your percussion ensemble can perform for the band or at other school and community events.

185. CAN – CAN

Jacques Offenbach
Arr. by Kevin Lepper

185. CAN – CAN

Jacques Offenbach
Arr. by Kevin Lepper

185. CAN – CAN

Jacques Offenbach
Arr. by Kevin Lepper

DUETS

Swing Low, Sweet Chariot and **La Bamba** are written as duets for woodwinds, brass, and keyboard percussion. These percussion parts can accompany two or more players playing the duet parts.

Rudiment Review

Flam Accent
(Eighth Notes)

The snare drum rudiment used in measures 11 and 15. Follow the sticking carefully.

186. SWING LOW, SWEET CHARIOT

African-American Spiritual

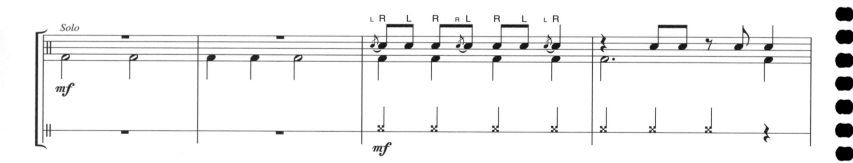

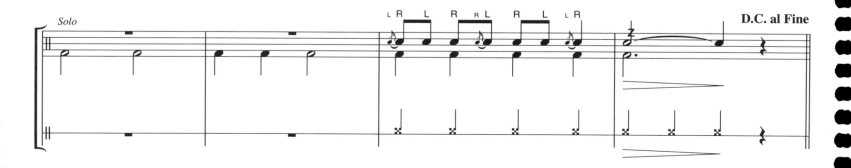

Rim Knock

Hold left stick with butt end facing out. Place tip of stick about 1/3 away from the rim and *knock* the butt end of the stick on the rim. A rim knock is usually written with an ✗ on the snare drum space. The regular notes are played on the drum head with the right hand.

187. LA BAMBA

Mexican Folk Song

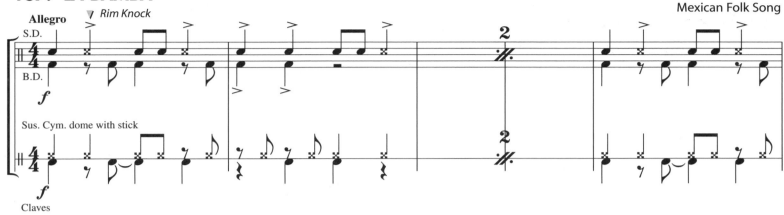

RUBANK® RUDIMENTAL STUDIES
and accompaniment for Full Band Scale and Arpeggio Studies

1. (Concert B♭ or Concert E♭ Major)

2. (Concert B♭ or Concert E♭ Major)

3. (Concert B♭ or Concert E♭ Major)

4. (Concert B♭ or Concert E♭ Major)

RUBANK® RUDIMENTAL STUDIES
and accompaniment for Full Band Scale and Arpeggio Studies

1. (Concert F or Concert A♭ Major)

2. (Concert F or Concert A♭ Major)

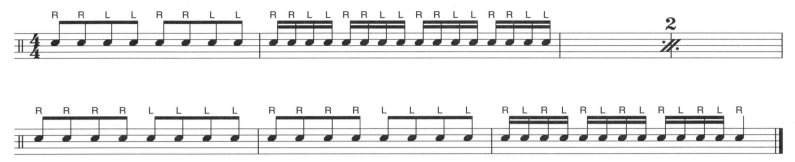

3. (Concert F or Concert A♭ Major)

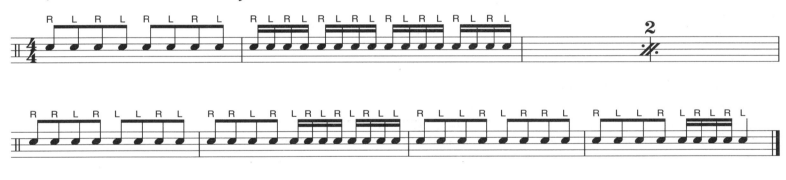

4. (Concert F or Concert A♭ Major)

RHYTHM STUDIES

RHYTHM STUDIES

CREATING MUSIC

THEORY

Composition

Composition is the art of writing original music. A composer often begins by creating a melody made up of individual **phrases**, like short musical "sentences." Some melodies have phrases that seem to answer or respond to "question" phrases, as in Beethoven's *Ode To Joy*. Play this melody and listen to how phrases 2 and 4 give slightly different answers to the same question (phrases 1 and 3).

1. ODE TO JOY

Ludwig van Beethoven

2. Q. AND A.
Write your own "answer" phrases in this melody.

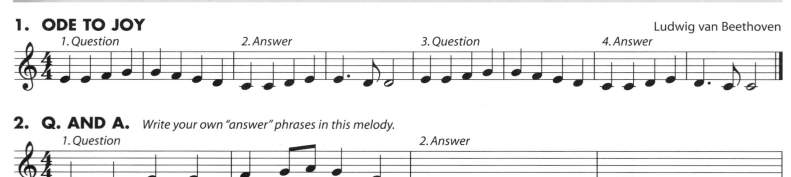

3. PHRASE BUILDERS
Write 4 different phrases using the rhythms below each staff.

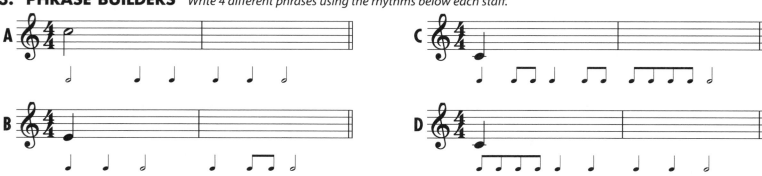

4. YOU NAME IT: _____

Pick phrase A, B, C, or D from above, and write it as the "Question" for phrases 1 and 3 below. Then write 2 different "Answers" for phrases 2 and 4.

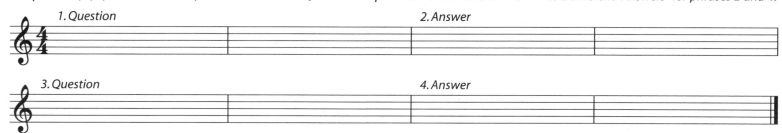

THEORY

Improvisation

Improvisation is the art of freely creating your own melody *as you play*. Use these notes to play your own melody (Line A), to go with the accompaniment (Line B).

5. INSTANT MELODY

Y ou can mark your progress through the book on this page. Fill in the stars as instructed by your band director.

ESSENTIAL ELEMENTS

STAR ACHIEVER

NAME_____

1.   Page 2–3, The Basics
2.   Page 5, EE Quiz, No. 13
3.   Page 6, EE Quiz, No. 19
4.   Page 7, EE Quiz, No. 26
5.   Page 8, EE Quiz, No. 32
6.   Page 10, EE Quiz, No. 45
7.   Page 12–13, Performance Spotlight
8.   Page 14, EE Quiz, No. 65
9.   Page 15, Essential Creativity, No. 72
10.   Page 17, EE Quiz, No. 84
11.   Page 17, Essential Creativity, No. 85
12.   Page 19, EE Quiz, No. 98
13.   Page 20, Essential Creativity, No. 104
14.   Page 21, No. 109

15.   Page 22, EE Quiz, No. 117
16.   Page 23, Performance Spotlight
17.   Page 24, EE Quiz, No. 125
18.   Page 26, Essential Creativity, No. 137
19.   Page 28, No. 149
20.   Page 28, EE Quiz, No. 151
21.   Page 29, Performance Spotlight
22.   Page 31, EE Quiz, No. 164
23.   Page 32, EE Quiz, No. 168
24.   Page 33, No. 174
25.   Page 35, EE Quiz, No. 181
26.   Page 36, Performance Spotlight
27.   Page 37, Performance Spotlight
28.   Page 38, Performance Spotlight

MUSIC — AN ESSENTIAL ELEMENT OF LIFE

SNARE DRUM INTERNATIONAL DRUM RUDIMENTS

All rudiments should be practiced: open (slow) to close (fast) and/or at an even moderate march tempo.

Instrument Care Reminders

Snare drums occasionally need tuning. Ask your teacher to help you tighten each tension rod equally using a drum key.

- Be careful not to over-tighten the head. It will break if the tension is too tight.
- Loosen the snare strainer at the end of each rehearsal.
- Cover all percussion instruments when not in use.
- Put sticks away in a storage area. Keep the percussion section neat!
- Sticks are the only things which should be placed on the snare drum. NEVER put or allow others to put objects on any percussion instrument.

Instrument courtesy of Yamaha Corporation of America, Band and Orchestral Division

I. ROLL RUDIMENTS

A. SINGLE STROKE RUDIMENTS

1. Single Stroke Roll

R L R L R L R L

2. Single Stroke Four

R L R L   R L R L
L R L R   L R L R

3. Single Stroke Seven

R L R L R L R
L R L R L R L

B. MULTIPLE BOUNCE ROLL RUDIMENTS

4. Multiple Bounce Roll

R R R R R R R R L L L L L L L L

5. Triple Stroke Roll

R R R L L L   R R R L L L

International Drum Rudiments courtesy of Percussion Arts Society
Copyright © 1984

SNARE DRUM INTERNATIONAL DRUM RUDIMENTS

C. DOUBLE STROKE OPEN ROLL RUDIMENTS

6. Double Stroke Open Roll

R R R L L L R R L L

7. Five Stroke Roll

R   R   L   L

8. Six Stroke Roll

R   L   R   L
L   R   L   R

9. Seven Stroke Roll

R   R   L   L
L   R   L   R

10. Nine Stroke Roll

R   R   L   L

11. Ten Stroke Roll

R   R L   R   R L
L   L R   L   L R

12. Eleven Stroke Roll

R   R L   R   R L
L   L R   L   L R

13. Thirteen Stroke Roll

R   R   L   L

14. Fifteen Stroke Roll

R   L   R   L
L   R   L   R

15. Seventeen Stroke Roll

R   R   L   L

II. DIDDLE RUDIMENTS

16. Single Paradiddle

R L R R L R L L

17. Double Paradiddle

R L R L R R L R L R L L

18. Triple Paradiddle

R L R L R L R R L R L R L R L L

19. Single Paradiddle-Diddle

R L R R L L R L R R L L
L R L L R R L R L L R R

SNARE DRUM INTERNATIONAL DRUM RUDIMENTS

III. FLAM RUDIMENTS

20. Flam

21. Flam Accent

22. Flam Tap

23. Flamacue

24. Flam Paradiddle

25. Single Flamed Mill

26. Flam Paradiddle-Diddle

27. Pataflafla
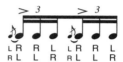

28. Swiss Army Triplet

29. Inverted Flam Tap

30. Flam Drag

IV. DRAG RUDIMENTS

31. Drag

32. Single Drag Tap

33. Double Drag Tap

34. Lesson 25

35. Single Dragadiddle

36. Drag Paradiddle #1

37. Drag Paradiddle #2

38. Single Ratamacue

39. Double Ratamacue

40. Triple Ratamacue

REFERENCE INDEX

REFERENCE INDEX FOR PERCUSSION

Definitions (pg.)

ESSENTIAL ELEMENTS
FOR BAND

COMPREHENSIVE BAND METHOD

TIM LAUTZENHEISER
JOHN HIGGINS
CHARLES MENGHINI
PAUL LAVENDER
TOM C. RHODES
DON BIERSCHENK

Percussion consultant and editor
WILL RAPP

HAL•LEONARD® CORPORATION

ESSENTIAL ELEMENTS
FOR BAND

COMPREHENSIVE BAND METHOD

TIM LAUTZENHEISER JOHN HIGGINS CHARLES MENGHINI
PAUL LAVENDER TOM C. RHODES DON BIERSCHENK

Percussion consultant and editor
WILL RAPP

Band is… **M**aking music with a family of lifelong friends.
Understanding how commitment and dedication lead to success.
Sharing the joy and rewards of working together.
Individuals who develop self-confidence.
Creativity—expressing yourself in a universal language.
Band is…**MUSIC!**

Strike up the band,
Tim Lautzenheiser

HISTORY OF KEYBOARD PERCUSSION

Keyboard percussion instruments were known to exist around 3500 B.C. in the Orient. The xylophone is probably the oldest keyboard percussion instrument, while the vibraphone is a 20th century American invention.

The initial purpose of the glockenspiel, or orchestra bells, was to aid 13th century Dutch bell masters in tuning their tower carillons. The similar bell lyra was used by German armies after 1870. Today, keyboard percussion instruments are used in marching bands, concert bands and orchestras.

Saint-Saëns, Mahler, Tchaikovsky and Hovhaness are all important composers who have included keyboard percussion instruments in their writing.

Common keyboard percussion instruments include orchestra bells, xylophone, marimba, vibraphone and chimes. Clair Musser, Milt Jackson, Gary Burton and Lionel Hampton are famous keyboard percussionists.

ISBN 978-0-634-00327-1

HAL•LEONARD®
CORPORATION
7777 W. BLUEMOUND RD. P.O. BOX 13819 MILWAUKEE, WI 53213

THE BASICS

Posture

Stand near your instrument, and always keep your:
- Spine straight and tall
- Shoulders back and relaxed
- Feet flat on the floor

Matched Grip (A Natural Stick Position)

Every percussion instrument requiring sticks or mallets can be played with this basic grip. Both sticks or mallets are held exactly the same "matched" way.

- Place the mallets in front of you with the heads pointing forward.
- Extend your right hand as if shaking hands with someone.
- Pick up the right mallet with your thumb and index finger about 1/3 from the end of the stick.
- The curve of your index finger's top knuckle and the thumb hold the mallet in place.
- Gently curve your other fingerings around the mallet.
- Check to be sure the mallet is cradled in the palm of your hand.
- Turn your hand palm-down to a comfortable resting position as shown:
- Follow the same procedure for your left hand.

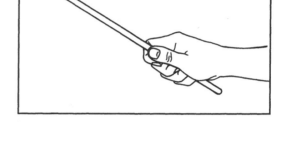

Practice & Performance Position

- Stand in front of a flat surface about waist high.
- Place the heads of the sticks on the surface. Make sure that your wrists are not turned in or out.
- The mallets should create the outline of a slice of pie as you look at them.
- When playing your instrument, hold mallets 6-8 inches from the surface. Using your wrist, throw the mallet near the center of one key. Pull the sound out of the keys by bringing the mallet up after the strike.

Taking Care of Your Instruments

- Cover all percussion instruments when they are not being used.
- Put mallets away in a storage area. Keep the percussion section neat!
- Mallets are the only things which should be placed on your instrument. NEVER put or allow others to put objects on any percussion instrument.

Sticking Work-Outs (Legato Stroke)

R = Right hand mallet
L = Left hand mallet

Find the largest key at the left end of the instrument. Play the following work-out keeping an even pulse. Start with your mallet in the up position. The down/up arrows indicate the speed of the mallet when playing *legato strokes*.

● = Strike near the center of the key.

Getting It Together

Step 1 Stand in a comfortable position near the instrument. The raised keys should be pointing away from you.

Step 2 If you are playing orchestra bells, set the instrument on a table or stand about waist high. The larger keys should be on the left.

Step 3 Adjust the music stand to about eye level. This enables you to easily read the music and watch your teacher.

Step 4 Hold the mallets as described on page 2.

Step 5 The sequence of keys for all keyboard percussion instruments is the same as the piano. Notice that the sequence is in alphabetical order from A–G. This diagram of orchestra bells will help you find **F**. Ask your teacher to help you play **F** if you are playing a different keyboard percussion instrument.

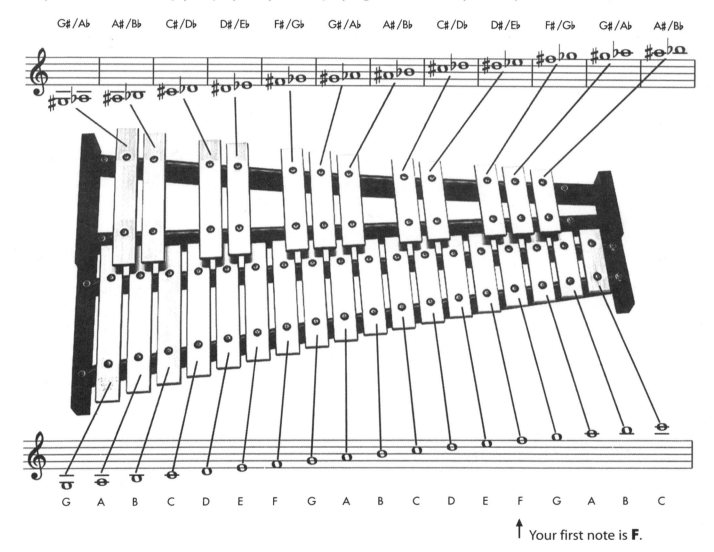

↑ Your first note is **F**.

READING MUSIC
Identify and draw each of these symbols:

Music Staff

The **music staff** has 5 lines and 4 spaces where notes and rests are written.

Ledger Lines

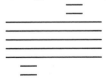

Ledger lines extend the music staff. Notes on ledger lines can be above or below the staff.

Measures & Bar Lines

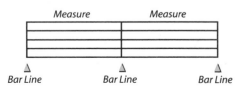

Bar lines divide the music staff into **measures**.

Long Tone

As wind players learn Long Tones, keyboard percussionists use a special Legato Stroke.

1. THE FIRST NOTE

Play a legato stroke for each new note.

F

| | REST | | REST |

The Beat

The **beat** is the pulse of music, and like your heartbeat it should remain very steady. Counting aloud and foot-tapping help us maintain a steady beat. Tap your foot **down** on each number and **up** on each "&."

One beat = 1 &
↓ ↑

Notes And Rests

Notes tell us how high or low to play by their placement on a line or space of the music staff, and how long to play by their shape. **Rests** tell us to count silent beats.

♩ **Quarter Note** = **1 beat**

𝄽 **Quarter Rest** = **1 silent beat**

Alternate Sticking

A hand to hand sticking pattern usually beginning with the right hand.

2. COUNT AND PLAY – Alternate Sticking

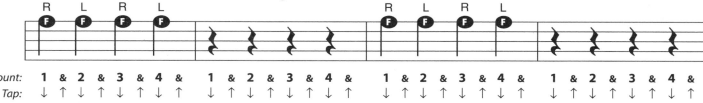

Count: **1** & **2** & **3** & **4** & **1** & **2** & **3** & **4** & **1** & **2** & **3** & **4** & **1** & **2** & **3** & **4** &
Tap: ↓ ↑ ↓ ↑ ↓ ↑ ↓ ↑ ↓ ↑ ↓ ↑ ↓ ↑ ↓ ↑ ↓ ↑ ↓ ↑ ↓ ↑ ↓ ↑ ↓ ↑ ↓ ↑ ↓ ↑ ↓ ↑

3. A NEW NOTE

This note is "E♭ (E-flat)."

E♭

| | REST | | REST |

4. TWO'S A TEAM

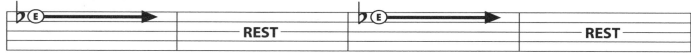

Count & Tap: **1** & **2** & **3** & **4** & **1** & **2** & **3** & **4** & **1** & **2** & **3** & **4** & **1** & **2** & **3** & **4** &

5. HEADING DOWN

D

| | REST | | REST |

Double Sticking

A pattern in which two consecutive notes are played with the same hand (RRLL, RRLL). This pattern may begin with either a double right or double left sticking.

6. MOVING ON UP – Double Sticking

Count & Tap: **1** & **2** & **3** & **4** & **1** & **2** & **3** & **4** & **1** & **2** & **3** & **4** & **1** & **2** & **3** & **4** &

Double Bar indicates the end of a piece of music.

Repeat Sign Without stopping, play once again from the beginning.

7. THE LONG HAUL
Double Bar

C

C ⟶ | REST | C ⟶ | REST |

8. FOUR BY FOUR – Alternate Sticking
Repeat Sign

R L R L R ... R L R L R ... R

C C C C | D ... | F F F F | ♭E ...

Count & Tap: 1 & 2 & 3 & 4 & | 1 & 2 & 3 & 4 & | 1 & 2 & 3 & 4 & | 1 & 2 & 3 & 4 &

9. TOUCHDOWN

B♭

♭B ⟶ | REST | ♭B ⟶ | REST |

10. THE FAB FIVE – Double Sticking

Remember!

R R L L R ... R R L L R

♭B ♭B ♭B ♭B | C ... | F F ♭E ♭E | D ...

1 & 2 & 3 & 4 & | 1 & 2 & 3 & 4 & | 1 & 2 & 3 & 4 & | 1 & 2 & 3 & 4 &

Treble Clef
(G Clef) indicates the position of note names on a music staff: Second line is G.

Time Signature
indicates how many beats per measure and what kind of note gets one beat.

4/4 = **4 beats** per measure
= **Quarter** note gets one beat

Note Names
Each note is on a line or space of the staff. These note names are indicated by the Treble Clef.

C D E F G A B C D E F

THEORY

Sharp ♯ raises the note and remains in effect for the entire measure.

Flat ♭ lowers the note and remains in effect for the entire measure.

Natural ♮ cancels a flat (♭) or sharp (♯) and remains in effect for the entire measure.

11. READING THE NOTES
Compare this to exercise 10, THE FAB FIVE.

1 & 2 & 3 & 4 & | 1 & 2 & 3 & 4 & | 1 & 2 & 3 & 4 & | 1 & 2 & 3 & 4 &

12. FIRST FLIGHT

Practice! 12, 13, 14 good luck

13. ESSENTIAL ELEMENTS QUIZ
Fill in the remaining note names before playing.

B♭ C D ___ ___ ___ ___ ___ ___ ___

Notes In Review

F   Eb   D   C   Bb

14. ROLLING ALONG Alternate Sticking

Go to the next line. ▾

Double Bar ▾

Half Note

♩ ⟶ = 2 Beats

1 & 2 &

Half Rest

▬ = 2 Silent Beats

▬ = 𝄽 𝄽

1 & 2 &

15. RHYTHM RAP *Clap the rhythm while counting and tapping.*

Clap

Repeat Sign ▾

1 & 2 & 3 & 4 & 1 & 2 & 3 & 4 & 1 & 2 & 3 & 4 & 1 & 2 & 3 & 4 & 1 & 2 & 3 & 4 & 1 & 2 & 3 & 4 &

Combination Sticking A sticking pattern that combines both alternate and double sticking.

16. THE HALF COUNTS Combination Sticking

R   L   L   R   R   L   L   R   R   L   R   L   R

1 & 2 & 3 & 4 & 1 & 2 & 3 & 4 & 1 & 2 & 3 & 4 & 1 & 2 & 3 & 4 & 1 & 2 & 3 & 4 & 1 & 2 & 3 & 4 &

17. HOT CROSS BUNS

R   L   R   R   L   R   R   L   R   L   R   L   R   L   R   L   R

Right Hand Lead A sticking pattern that begins with the right hand and keeps the right hand on strong beats.

18. GO TELL AUNT RHODIE Right Hand Lead

American Folk Song

R   R   L   R   R   R   R   L   R   L   R   R   R   L   R   R   R   L   R   L   R

19. ESSENTIAL ELEMENTS QUIZ *Using the note names and rhythms below, draw your notes on the staff before playing.*

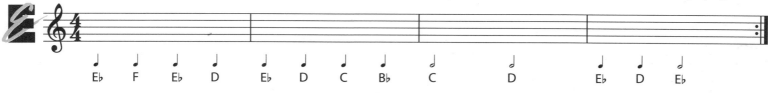

♩   ♩   ♩   ♩   ♩   ♩   ♩   ♩   𝅗𝅥   𝅗𝅥   ♩   ♩   ♩

Eb   F   Eb   D   Eb   D   C   Bb   C   D   Eb   D   Eb

8

Fermata 🎵 Hold the note (or rest) longer than normal.

27. REACHING HIGHER – New Note.

Fermata ▽

28. AU CLAIRE DE LA LUNE Left Hand Lead

French Folk Song

L R L R L R   *sim.*

29. REMIX

Harmony   Two or more notes played together. Each combination forms a *chord*.

30. LONDON BRIDGE – Duet

English Folk Song

A
B

Austrian composer **Wolfgang Amadeus Mozart** (1756–1791) was a child prodigy who started playing professionally at age six, and lived during the time of the American Revolution. Mozart's music is melodic and imaginative. He wrote more than 600 compositions during his short life, including a piano piece based on the famous song, "Twinkle, Twinkle, Little Star."

31. A MOZART MELODY Double Sticking

Adaptation

R R R L L R R L   *sim.*

32. ESSENTIAL ELEMENTS QUIZ *Draw these symbols where they belong and write in the note names before you play:*

9

33. DEEP POCKETS – New Note

A

△ A

34. DOODLE ALL DAY Combination Sticking

35. JUMP ROPE

Pick-Up Notes   One or more notes that come before the first *full* measure. The beats of Pick-Up Notes are subtracted from the last measure.

36. A-TISKET, A-TASKET Combination Sticking

4   1 & 2 & 3 & 4   1 & 2 & 3 &

Dynamics   *f* – forte (play loudly)   *mf* – mezzo forte (play moderately loud)   *p* – piano (play softly)
The higher you lift the mallet, the louder the note will sound.

37. LOUD AND SOFT

38. JINGLE BELLS

J. S. Pierpont

39. MY DREYDL

Traditional Hanukkah Song

Eighth Notes

Each Eighth Note = ½ Beat
2 Eighth Notes = 1 Beat
Play on down and up taps.
1   &

1   &   2   &

Two or more Eighth Notes have a *beam* across the stems.

▼ *Beam*
=

40. RHYTHM RAP *Clap the rhythm while counting and tapping.*

Clap
1 & 2 & 3 & 4 &   1 & 2 & 3 & 4 &   1 & 2 & 3 & 4 &   1 & 2 & 3 & 4 &

41. EIGHTH NOTE JAM

1 & 2 & 3 & 4 &   1 & 2 & 3 & 4 &   1 & 2 & 3 & 4 &   1 & 2 & 3 & 4 &

42. SKIP TO MY LOU   Alternate Sticking

American Folk Song

R L R L R L   R   L   R   *sim.*

mf

R   L   R   L   R   L   R

43. LONG, LONG AGO

p

44. OH, SUSANNA

Stephen Collins Foster

f

HISTORY

Italian composer **Gioacchino Rossini** (1792–1868) began composing as a teenager and was very proficient on the piano, viola and horn. He wrote "William Tell" at age 37 as the last of his forty operas, and its familiar theme is still heard today on radio and television.

45. ESSENTIAL ELEMENTS QUIZ — WILLIAM TELL

Gioacchino Rossini

mf

f

2/4 Time Signature

= **2 beats** per measure
= **Quarter** note gets one beat

Conducting

Practice conducting this two-beat pattern.

46. RHYTHM RAP

1 & 2 & 1 & 2 & 1 & 2 & 1 & 2 & 1 & 2 & 1 & 2 & 1 & 2 & 1 & 2 &

47. TWO BY TWO

1 & 2 & 1 & 2 & 1 & 2 & 1 & 2 & 1 & 2 & 1 & 2 & 1 & 2 & 1 & 2 &

Tempo Markings

Tempo is the speed of music. Tempo markings are usually written above the staff, in Italian.
Allegro – Fast tempo   **Moderato** – Medium tempo   **Andante** – Slower walking tempo

48. HIGH SCHOOL CADETS – March

John Philip Sousa

Reproduced by Permission of Boosey & Hawkes Music Publishers Ltd.

49. HEY, HO! NOBODY'S HOME – New Note

Dynamics

Crescendo (gradually louder)   *Decrescendo* or *Diminuendo* (gradually softer)

50. CLAP THE DYNAMICS

51. PLAY THE DYNAMICS

PERFORMANCE SPOTLIGHT

52. PERFORMANCE WARM-UPS

TONE BUILDER

RHYTHM ETUDE Combination Sticking

RHYTHM RAP

Clap

Stomp!

CHORALE

Andante

Melodic Sticking   An approach that combines all the various stickings to create the best performance of the melodic line.

53. AURA LEE – Duet or Band Arrangement   Melodic Sticking with Doublings

(Part A = Melody, Part B = Harmony)

George R. Poulton

Andante

sim.

54. FRÈRE JACQUES – Round   *(When group A reaches ② , group B begins at ①)*

Melodic Sticking

Moderato

French Folk Song

PERFORMANCE SPOTLIGHT

55. WHEN THE SAINTS GO MARCHING IN – Band Arrangement

Arr. by John Higgins

56. OLD MACDONALD HAD A BAND – Section Feature

57. ODE TO JOY (from Symphony No. 9)

Ludwig van Beethoven
Arr. by John Higgins

58. HARD ROCK BLUES – Encore

John Higgins

14

Tie   A curved line connecting notes of the same pitch. Play one note for the combined counts of the tied notes.    = 2 Beats

59. FIT TO BE TIED

2 beats △

60. ALOUETTE

French-Canadian Folk Song

3 beats △

Dotted Half Note

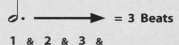   = 3 Beats   **Dot**   A dot adds half the value of the note.   

1 & 2 & 3 &   2 beats + 1 beat = 3 beats

61. ALOUETTE – THE SEQUEL

French-Canadian Folk Song

62. CAMPTOWN RACES

Allegro   Stephen Collins Foster

mf

63. NEW DIRECTIONS – New Note

F

△ F

64. THE NOBLES

3 beats △

65. ESSENTIAL ELEMENTS QUIZ

$\frac{3}{4}$ Time Signature

$\frac{3}{4}$ = **3 beats** per measure
= **Quarter** note gets one beat

Conducting

Practice conducting this three-beat pattern.

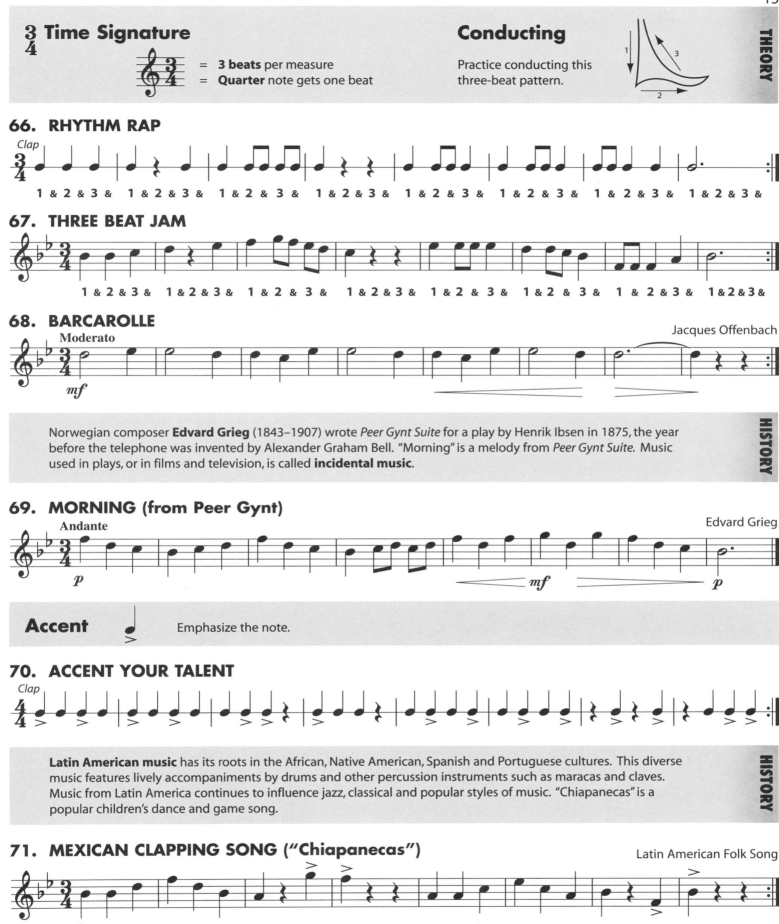

66. RHYTHM RAP

Clap

1 & 2 & 3 &   1 & 2 & 3 &   1 & 2 & 3 &   1 & 2 & 3 &   1 & 2 & 3 &   1 & 2 & 3 &   1 & 2 & 3 &   1 & 2 & 3 &

67. THREE BEAT JAM

1 & 2 & 3 &   1 & 2 & 3 &   1 & 2 & 3 &   1 & 2 & 3 &   1 & 2 & 3 &   1 & 2 & 3 &   1 & 2 & 3 &   1 & 2 & 3 &

68. BARCAROLLE

Jacques Offenbach

Moderato

mf

HISTORY

Norwegian composer **Edvard Grieg** (1843–1907) wrote *Peer Gynt Suite* for a play by Henrik Ibsen in 1875, the year before the telephone was invented by Alexander Graham Bell. "Morning" is a melody from *Peer Gynt Suite*. Music used in plays, or in films and television, is called **incidental music**.

69. MORNING (from Peer Gynt)

Edvard Grieg

Andante

p   mf   p

Accent   Emphasize the note.

70. ACCENT YOUR TALENT

Clap

HISTORY

Latin American music has its roots in the African, Native American, Spanish and Portuguese cultures. This diverse music features lively accompaniments by drums and other percussion instruments such as maracas and claves. Music from Latin America continues to influence jazz, classical and popular styles of music. "Chiapanecas" is a popular children's dance and game song.

71. MEXICAN CLAPPING SONG ("Chiapanecas")

Latin American Folk Song

f

72. ESSENTIAL CREATIVITY

Compose your own music for measures 3 and 4 using this rhythm:

16

THEORY

Accidental

Any sharp, flat or natural sign which appears in the music without being in the key signature is called an **accidental**.

Flat ♭

A **flat** sign lowers the pitch of a note by a half-step. The note A-flat sounds a half-step below A, and all A's become A-flats for the rest of the measure where they occur.

73. HOT MUFFINS – New Note

Flat applies to all A's in measure.

74. COSSACK DANCE

75. BASIC BLUES – New Note

Flat applies to all A's in measure.

THEORY

New Key Signature

This Key Signature indicates the *Key of* E♭ – play all B's as B-flats, all E's as E-flats, and all A's as A-flats.

1st & 2nd Endings

Play through the 1st Ending. Then play the repeated section of music, **skipping** the 1st Ending and playing the 2nd Ending.

76. HIGH FLYING

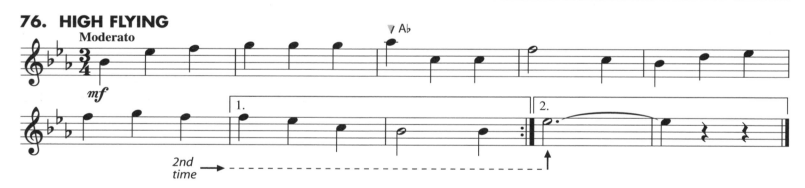

HISTORY

Japanese folk music actually has its origins in ancient China. "Sakura, Sakura" was performed on instruments such as the **koto**, a 13-string instrument that is more than 4000 years old, and the **shakuhachi** or bamboo flute. The unique sound of this ancient Japanese melody results from the pentatonic (or five-note) sequence used in this tonal system.

77. SAKURA, SAKURA – Band Arrangement

Japanese Folk Song
Arr. by John Higgins

78. UP ON A HOUSETOP

79. JOLLY OLD ST. NICK – Duet

See page 9 for additional holiday music, MY DREYDL and JINGLE BELLS.

80. THE BIG AIRSTREAM – New Note

81. WALTZ THEME

Franz Lehar

© Glocken Verlag Ltd., London
Reproduced by Permission

82. AIR TIME

83. DOWN BY THE STATION

84. ESSENTIAL ELEMENTS QUIZ

85. ESSENTIAL CREATIVITY   *Using these notes, improvise your own rhythms:*

DAILY WARM-UPS

WORK-OUTS FOR TONE & TECHNIQUE

86. TONE BUILDER

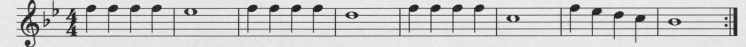

87. RHYTHM BUILDER

88. TECHNIQUE TRAX

89. CHORALE *(Adapted from Cantata 147)*

Johann Sebastian Bach

THEORY

Theme and Variations

A musical form featuring a **theme**, or primary melody, followed by **variations**, or altered versions of the theme.

90. VARIATIONS ON A FAMILIAR THEME

D.C. al Fine

At the **D.C. al Fine** play again from the beginning, stopping at **Fine** *(fee'- nay)*.
D.C. is the abbreviation for **Da Capo**, or "to the beginning," and **Fine** means "the end."

91. BANANA BOAT SONG

Caribbean Folk Song

Natural ♮   A **natural** sign cancels a flat (♭) or sharp (♯) and remains in effect for the entire measure.

92. RAZOR'S EDGE – New Note

E

△ E♮

93. THE MUSIC BOX

Moderato

p   △ E

African-American spirituals originated in the 1700's, midway through the period of slavery in the United States. One of the largest categories of true American folk music, these primarily religious songs were sung and passed on for generations without being written down. The first collection of spirituals was published in 1867, four years after The Emancipation Proclamation was signed into law.

HISTORY

94. EZEKIEL SAW THE WHEEL

African-American Spiritual

Allegro

f

95. SMOOTH OPERATOR

96. GLIDING ALONG

Ragtime is an American music style that was popular from the 1890's until the time of World War I. This early form of jazz brought fame to pianists like "Jelly Roll" Morton and Scott Joplin, who wrote "The Entertainer" and "Maple Leaf Rag." Surprisingly, the style was incorporated into some orchestral music by Igor Stravinsky and Claude Debussy. The trombones now learn to play a *glissando*, a technique used in ragtime and other styles of music.

HISTORY

97. TROMBONE RAG

Allegro

f

98. ESSENTIAL ELEMENTS QUIZ

Andante   **Fine**   **D.C. al Fine**

p

20

99. TAKE THE LEAD – New Note

A

△ A   △ E♭

THEORY

Phrase   A musical "sentence" which is often 2 or 4 measures long.

100. THE COLD WIND

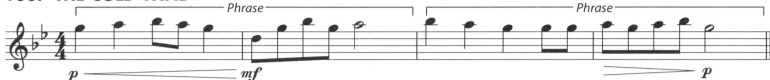

Phrase   Phrase

p ——— *mf*   *p*

101. PHRASEOLOGY

f   △ A♭   *p*   *f*

THEORY

New Key Signature
This **Key Signature** indicates the *Key of F* – play all B's as B-flats.

Multiple Measure Rest
The number above the staff tells you how many full measures to rest. Count each measure of rest in sequence:

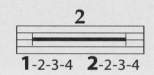

1-2-3-4   **2**-2-3-4

Roll   Rapidly alternate single strokes as smoothly as possible. Release the roll on the tied note or final beat with the same hand that started the roll. Rolls are usually found in xylophone and marimba music.

102. SATIN LATIN

Allegro

mf   △ Release   △ E   **2**   **1**-2-3-4 **2**-2-3-4

mf

HISTORY

German composer **Johann Sebastian Bach** (1685–1750) was part of a large family of famous musicians and became the most recognized composer of the Baroque era. Beginning as a choir member, Bach soon became an organist, a teacher, and a prolific composer, writing more than 600 masterworks. This *Minuet,* or dance in 3/4 time, was written as a teaching piece for use with an early form of the piano.

103. MINUET – Duet

Johann Sebastian Bach

Moderato

A   *mf*

B   *mf*

104. ESSENTIAL CREATIVITY

This melody can be played in 3/4 or 4/4. Pencil in either time signature, draw the bar lines and play. Now erase the bar lines and try the other time signature. Do the phrases sound different?

21

105. NATURALLY

Austrian composer **Franz Peter Schubert** (1797–1828) lived a shorter life than any other great composer, but he created an incredible amount of music: more than 600 art-songs (concert music for voice and accompaniment), ten symphonies, chamber music, operas, choral works and piano pieces. His "March Militaire" was originally a piano duet.

HISTORY

106. MARCH MILITAIRE – New Note

Franz Schubert

107. THE FLAT ZONE – New Note

108. ON TOP OF OLD SMOKEY

American Folk Song

Boogie-woogie is a style of the **blues**, and it was first recorded by pianist Clarence "Pine Top" Smith in 1928, one year after Charles Lindbergh's solo flight across the Atlantic. A form of jazz, blues music features altered notes and is usually written in 12-measure verses, like "Bottom Bass Boogie."

HISTORY

109. BOTTOM BASS BOOGIE – Duet

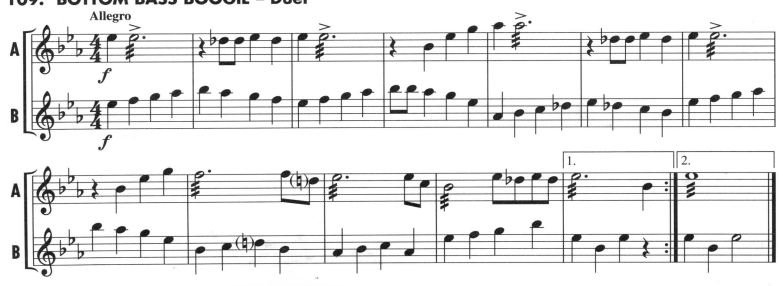

23

PERFORMANCE SPOTLIGHT

Solo with Piano Accompaniment

You can perform this solo with or without a piano accompanist. Play it for the band, the school or your family. It is part of **Symphony No. 9 ("From The New World")** by Czech composer **Antonin Dvorák** (1841–1904). He wrote it while visiting America in 1893, and was inspired to include melodies from American folksongs and spirituals. This is the **Largo** (or "very slow tempo") theme.

118. THEME FROM "NEW WORLD SYMPHONY"

Antonin Dvorák

Piano Accompaniment

Great musicians give encouragement to fellow performers. On this page, clarinetists learn their instruments' upper register in the "Grenadilla Gorilla Jumps" (named after the grenadilla wood used to make clarinets). Brass players learn lip slurs, a new warm-up pattern. The success of your band depends on everyone's effort and encouragement.

119. GRENADILLA GORILLA JUMP No. 1

120. JUMPIN' UP AND DOWN

121. GRENADILLA GORILLA JUMP No. 2 – New Note

C

122. JUMPIN' FOR JOY

123. GRENADILLA GORILLA JUMP No. 3

124. JUMPIN' JACKS

Interval

THEORY

The distance between two pitches is an **interval**. Starting with "1" on the lower note, count each line and space between the notes. The number of the higher note is the distance of the interval.

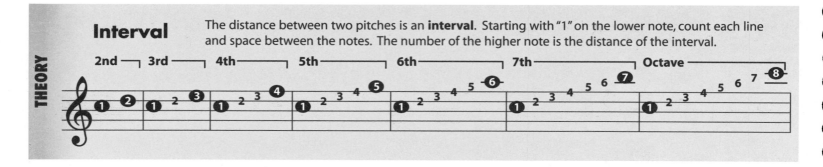

125. ESSENTIAL ELEMENTS QUIZ
Write in the numbers of the intervals, counting up from the lower notes.

Intervals: 2nd

126. GRENADILLA GORILLA JUMP No. 4

127. THREE IS THE COUNT

128. GRENADILLA GORILLA JUMP No. 5

129. TECHNIQUE TRAX

130. CROSSING OVER

△ *Low* E♭

Trio

A **trio** is a composition with three parts played together. Practice this trio with two other players and listen for the 3-part harmony.

131. KUM BAH YAH – Trio   *Always check the key signature.*

African Folk Song

Repeat Signs

Repeat the section of music enclosed by the **repeat signs**.
(If 1st and 2nd endings are used, they are played as usual — but go back only to the first repeat sign, not to the beginning.)

132. MICHAEL ROW THE BOAT ASHORE

African-American Spiritual

Andante

mf

1.

2.

133. AUSTRIAN WALTZ

Austrian Folk Song

Moderato

f

134. BOTANY BAY

Australian Folk Song

Allegro

mf

f

mf

THEORY

¢ Time Signature

¢ = **Common Time**

(Same as 4/4)

Conducting

Practice conducting this four-beat pattern.

1 4

2 3

135. TECHNIQUE TRAX *Practice at all dynamic levels.*

136. FINLANDIA

Jean Sibelius

Andante

p

mf

p

1.

2.

© Breitkopf & Haertel, Wiesbaden - Leipzig

137. ESSENTIAL CREATIVITY

Create your own variations by penciling in a dot and a flag to change the rhythm of any measure from ♩ ♩ *to* ♩. ♪

138. EASY GORILLA JUMPS

139. TECHNIQUE TRAX *Always check the key signature.*

140. MORE TECHNIQUE TRAX

141. GERMAN FOLK SONG

142. THE SAINTS GO MARCHIN' AGAIN

James Black and Katherine Purvis

143. LOWLAND GORILLA WALK

144. SMOOTH SAILING

145. MORE GORILLA JUMPS

146. FULL COVERAGE

THEORY

Scale

A **scale** is a sequence of notes in ascending or descending order. Like a musical "ladder," each step is the next consecutive note in the key. This scale is in your Key of B♭ (two flats), so the top and bottom notes are both B♭'s. The interval between the B♭'s is an octave.

147. CONCERT B♭ SCALE

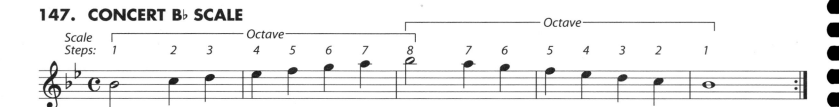

THEORY

Chord & Arpeggio

When two or more notes are played together, they form a **chord** or **harmony**. This B♭ chord is built from the 1st, 3rd and 5th steps of the B♭ scale. The 8th step is the same as the 1st, but it is an octave higher. An **arpeggio** is a "broken" chord whose notes are played individually.

148. IN HARMONY   *Divide the notes of the chords between band members and play together. Does the arpeggio sound like a chord?*

149. SCALE AND ARPEGGIO

HISTORY

Austrian composer **Franz Josef Haydn** (1732–1809) wrote 104 symphonies. Many of these works had nicknames and included brilliant, unique effects for their time. His Symphony No. 94 was named "The Surprise Symphony" because the soft second movement included a sudden loud dynamic, intended to wake up an often sleepy audience. Pay special attention to dynamics when you play this famous theme.

150. THEME FROM "SURPRISE SYMPHONY"

Franz Josef Haydn

151. ESSENTIAL ELEMENTS QUIZ – THE STREETS OF LAREDO

American Folk Song

Write in the note names before you play.

PERFORMANCE SPOTLIGHT

152. SCHOOL SPIRIT – Band Arrangement

W.T. Purdy
Arr. by John Higgins

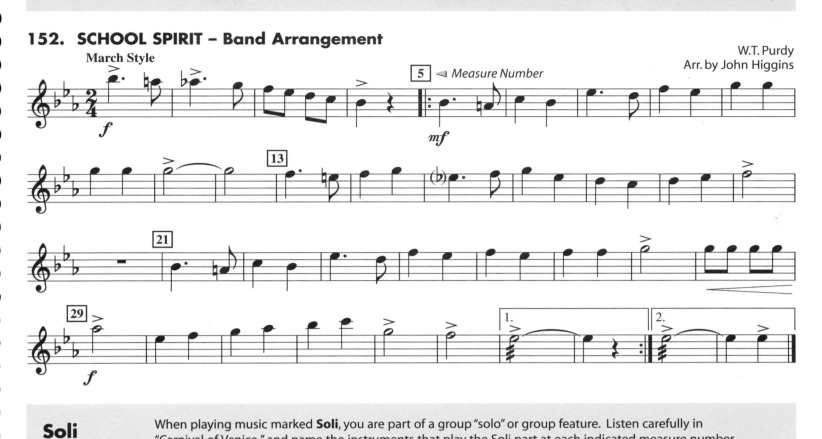

Soli

When playing music marked **Soli**, you are part of a group "solo" or group feature. Listen carefully in "Carnival of Venice," and name the instruments that play the Soli part at each indicated measure number.

153. CARNIVAL OF VENICE – Band Arrangement

Julius Benedict
Arr. by John Higgins

DAILY WARM-UPS

WORK-OUTS FOR TONE & TECHNIQUE

154. RANGE AND FLEXIBILITY BUILDER

155. TECHNIQUE TRAX

156. CHORALE

Johann Sebastian Bach

HISTORY

The traditional Hebrew melody "Hatikvah" has been Israel's national anthem since the nation's inception. At the Declaration of State in 1948, it was sung by the gathered assembly during the opening ceremony and played by members of the Palestine Symphony Orchestra at its conclusion.

157. HATIKVAH

Israeli National Anthem

Eighth Note & Eighth Rest

♪ = 1/2 beat of sound
♪ = 1/2 beat of silence

1 & 2 &   1 & 2 &

158. RHYTHM RAP

159. EIGHTH NOTE MARCH

160. MINUET

Johann Sebastian Bach

161. RHYTHM RAP

162. EIGHTH NOTES OFF THE BEAT

163. EIGHTH NOTE SCRAMBLE

164. ESSENTIAL ELEMENTS QUIZ

165. DANCING MELODY – New Note

Gb

American composer and conductor **John Philip Sousa** (1854–1932) wrote 136 marches. Known as "The March King," Sousa wrote *The Stars And Stripes Forever, Semper Fidelis, The Washington Post* and many other patriotic works. Sousa's band performed all over the country, and his fame helped boost the popularity of bands in America. Here is a melody from his famous *El Capitan* operetta and march.

166. EL CAPITAN

Allegro

John Philip Sousa

Reproduced by Permission of Boosey & Hawkes Music Publishers Ltd.

"O Canada," formerly known as the "National Song," was first performed during 1880 in French Canada. Robert Stanley Weir translated the English language version in 1908, but it was not adopted as the national anthem of Canada until 1980, one hundred years after its premiere.

167. O CANADA

Maestoso (Majestically)

Calixa Lavallee, l'Hon. Judge Routhier and Justice R.S. Weir

168. ESSENTIAL ELEMENTS QUIZ – METER MANIA

Count and clap before playing. Can you conduct this?

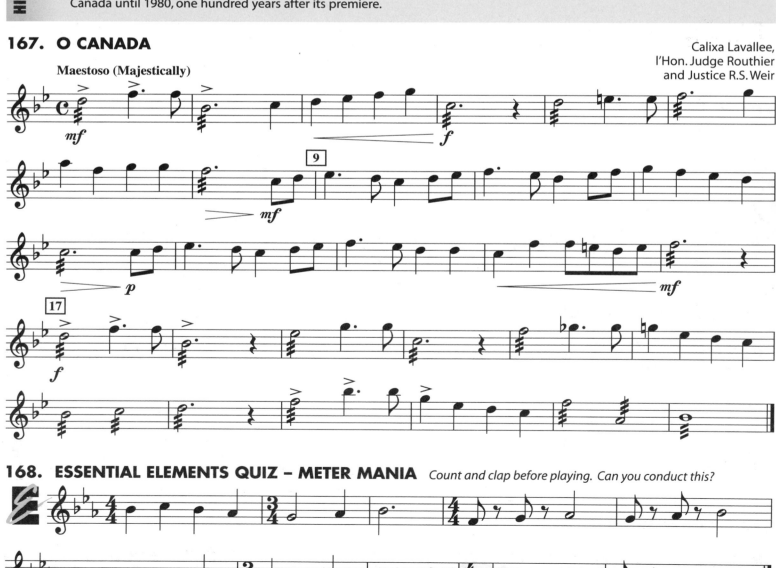

Enharmonics

Two notes that are written differently, but sound the same (and played with the same fingering) are called **enharmonics**. Your note chart on page 3 shows the enharmonic notes for your instrument.

On a piano keyboard, each black key is both a flat and a sharp:

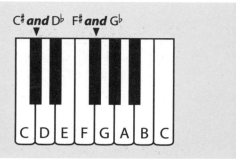

169. SNAKE CHARMER

△ G♭   △ F#

170. DARK SHADOWS

△ Pick-up note

171. CLOSE ENCOUNTERS

△ C#   △ D♭

172. MARCH SLAV

Peter Illyich Tchaikovsky

173. NOTES IN DISGUISE

Chromatic Notes

Chromatic notes are altered with sharps, flats and natural signs which are not in the key signature. The smallest distance between two notes is a half-step, and a scale made up of consecutive half-steps is called a **chromatic scale**.

174. HALF-STEPPIN'

French composer **Camille Saint-Saëns** (1835–1921) wrote music for virtually every medium: operas, suites, symphonies and chamber works. The "Egyptian Dance" is one of the main themes from his famous opera *Samson et Delilah*. The opera was written in the same year that Thomas Edison invented the phonograph—1877.

175. EGYPTIAN DANCE *Watch for enharmonics.*

Camille Saint-Saëns

176. SILVER MOON BOAT

Chinese Folk Song

German composer **Ludwig van Beethoven** (1770–1827) is considered to be one of the world's greatest composers, despite becoming completely deaf in 1802. Although he could not hear his music the way we can, he could "hear" it in his mind. As a testament to his greatness, his Symphony No. 9 (p. 13) was performed as the finale to the ceremony celebrating the reunification of Germany in 1990. This is the theme from his Symphony No. 7, second movement.

177. THEME FROM SYMPHONY NO. 7 – Duet

Ludwig van Beethoven

Russian composer **Peter Illyich Tchaikovsky** (1840–1893) wrote six symphonies and hundreds of other works including *The Nutcracker* ballet. He was a master at writing brilliant settings of folk music, and his original melodies are among the most popular of all time. His *1812 Overture* and *Capriccio Italien* were both written in 1880, the year after Thomas Edison developed the practical electric light bulb.

178. CAPRICCIO ITALIEN *Always check the key signature.*

Peter Illyich Tchaikovsky

179. AMERICAN PATROL

F.W. Meacham

180. WAYFARING STRANGER

African-American Spiritual

△ *Low* B♭

181. ESSENTIAL ELEMENTS QUIZ – SCALE COUNTING CONQUEST

PERFORMANCE SPOTLIGHT

182. AMERICA THE BEAUTIFUL – Band Arrangement

Samuel A. Ward
Arr. by John Higgins

183. LA CUCARACHA – Band Arrangement

Latin American Folk Song
Arr. by John Higgins

PERFORMANCE SPOTLIGHT

184. THEME FROM 1812 OVERTURE – Band Arrangement

Peter Illyich Tchaikovsky
Arr. by John Higgins

PERFORMANCE SPOTLIGHT

Solo for Percussion Ensemble

Performing for an audience is an exciting part of being involved in music. Percussion ensembles provide a unique solo performing opportunity for all members of the percussion section. This percussion ensemble is written for 5 or more players. It is based on the famous "Can-Can" dance from Jacques Offenbach's operetta *Orpheus in the Underworld,* completed in 1858. Your percussion ensemble can perform for the band or at other school and community events.

185. CAN – CAN

Jacques Offenbach
Arr. by Kevin Lepper

DUETS

Here is an opportunity to get together with a friend and enjoy playing music. The other player does not have to play the same instrument as you. Try to exactly match each other's rhythm, pitch and tone quality. Eventually, it may begin to sound like the two parts are being played by one person! Later, try switching parts.

186. SWING LOW, SWEET CHARIOT – Duet

African-American Spiritual

187. LA BAMBA – Duet

Mexican Folk Song

RUBANK® SCALE AND ARPEGGIO STUDIES

KEY OF Bb   *In this key signature, play all Bb's and Eb's.*

KEY OF Eb   *In this key signature, play all Bb's, Eb's and Ab's.*

RUBANK® SCALE AND ARPEGGIO STUDIES

KEY OF F *In this key signature, play all B♭'s.*

1.

2.

3.

4.

KEY OF A♭ *In this key signature, play all B♭'s, E♭'s, A♭'s and D♭'s.*

1.

2.

3.

4.

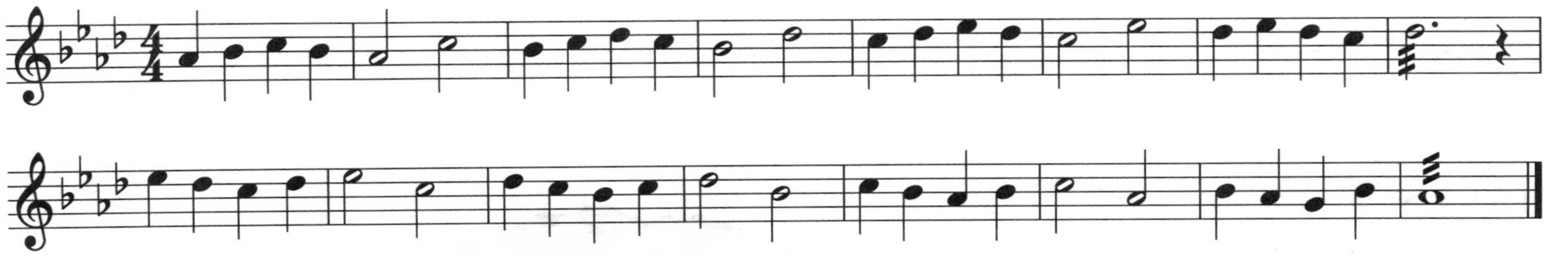

RHYTHM STUDIES

RHYTHM STUDIES

44

CREATING MUSIC

THEORY

Composition

Composition is the art of writing original music. A composer often begins by creating a melody made up of individual **phrases**, like short musical "sentences." Some melodies have phrases that seem to answer or respond to "question" phrases, as in Beethoven's *Ode To Joy*. Play this melody and listen to how phrases 2 and 4 give slightly different answers to the same question (phrases 1 and 3).

1. ODE TO JOY

Ludwig van Beethoven

2. Q. AND A.   *Write your own "answer" phrases in this melody.*

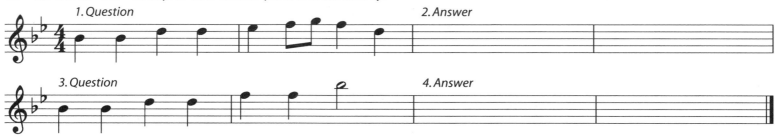

3. PHRASE BUILDERS   *Write 4 different phrases using the rhythms below each staff.*

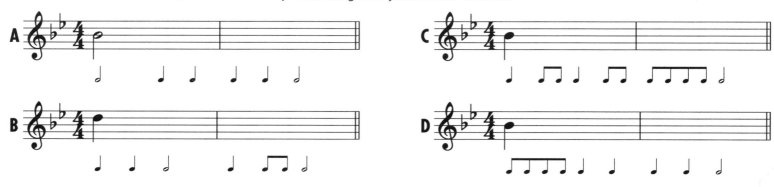

4. YOU NAME IT: _____

Pick phrase A, B, C, or D from above, and write it as the "Question" for phrases 1 and 3 below. Then write 2 different "Answers" for phrases 2 and 4.

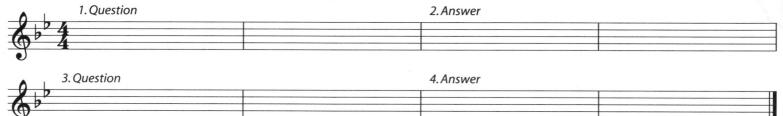

THEORY

Improvisation

Improvisation is the art of freely creating your own melody *as you play*. Use these notes to play your own melody (Line A), to go with the accompaniment (Line B).

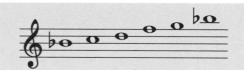

5. INSTANT MELODY

You can mark your progress through the book on this page. Fill in the stars as instructed by your band director.

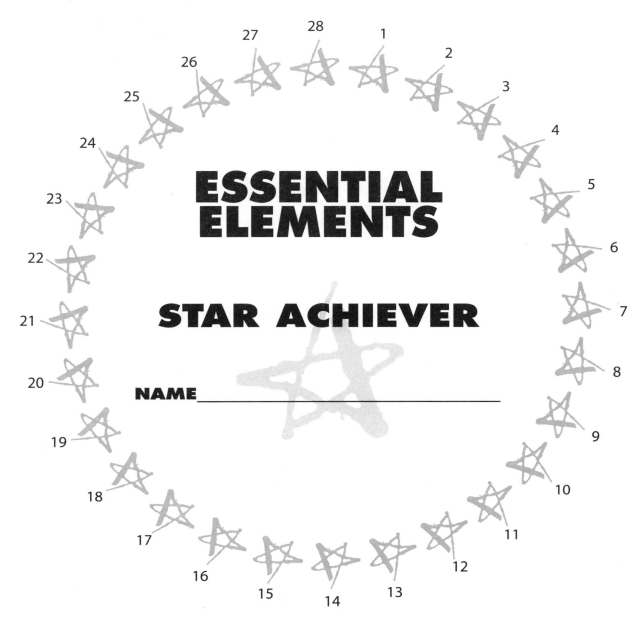

ESSENTIAL ELEMENTS

STAR ACHIEVER

NAME_____

1. Page 2–3, The Basics
2. Page 5, EE Quiz, No. 13
3. Page 6, EE Quiz, No. 19
4. Page 7, EE Quiz, No. 26
5. Page 8, EE Quiz, No. 32
6. Page 10, EE Quiz, No. 45
7. Page 12–13, Performance Spotlight
8. Page 14, EE Quiz, No. 65
9. Page 15, Essential Creativity, No. 72
10. Page 17, EE Quiz, No. 84
11. Page 17, Essential Creativity, No. 85
12. Page 19, EE Quiz, No. 98
13. Page 20, Essential Creativity, No. 104
14. Page 21, No. 109

15. Page 22, EE Quiz, No. 117
16. Page 23, Performance Spotlight
17. Page 24, EE Quiz, No. 125
18. Page 26, Essential Creativity, No. 137
19. Page 28, No. 149
20. Page 28, EE Quiz, No. 151
21. Page 29, Performance Spotlight
22. Page 31, EE Quiz, No. 164
23. Page 32, EE Quiz, No. 168
24. Page 33, No. 174
25. Page 35, EE Quiz, No. 181
26. Page 36, Performance Spotlight
27. Page 37, Performance Spotlight
28. Page 38, Performance Spotlight

MUSIC — AN ESSENTIAL ELEMENT OF LIFE

KEYBOARD PERCUSSION INSTRUMENTS

Each keyboard percussion instrument has a unique sound because of the materials used to create the instrument. Ranges may differ with some models of instruments.

Instrument Care Reminders

- Cover all percussion instruments when they are not being used.
- Put mallets away in a storage area. Keep the percussion section neat!
- Mallets are the only things which should be placed on your instrument. NEVER put or allow others to put objects on any percussion instrument.

BELLS (Orchestra Bells)

- Bars – metal alloy or steel
- Mallets – lexan (hard plastic), brass or hard rubber
- Range – 2 1/2 octaves
- Sounds 2 octaves higher than written

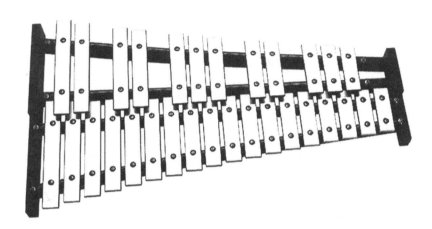

XYLOPHONE

- Bars – wooden or synthetic
- Mallets – hard rubber
- Range – 3 1/2 octaves
- Sounds 1 octave higher than written

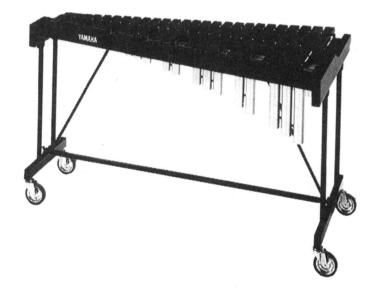

MARIMBA

- Bars – wooden (wider than xylophone bars) Resonating tube located below each bar
- Mallets – soft to medium rubber or yarn covered
- Range – 4 1/3 octaves (reads bass and treble clefs)
- Sounding pitch is the same as written pitch

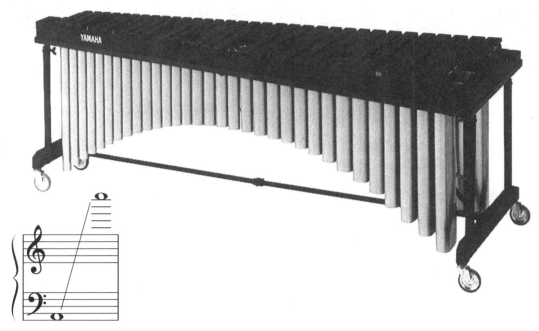

VIBRAPHONE

- Bars – metal alloy or aluminum Resonating tubes located below each bar Adjustable electric fans in each resonator create "vibrato" effect
- Mallets – yarn covered
- Range – 3 octaves
- Sounding pitch is the same as written pitch

CHIMES

- Bars – metal tubes
- Mallets – plastic, rawhide or wooden
- Range – 1 1/2 octaves
- Sounding pitch is the same as written pitch

Instruments and photos courtesy of Yamaha Corporation of America, Band and Orchestral Division

♪ REFERENCE INDEX

Definitions (pg.)

Composers

World Music

REFERENCE INDEX FOR PERCUSSION

Definitions (pg.)*

*These page numbers refer to the first section (percussion) of this book.

Notes

Notes

Notes